Social Work Practice Placements

SAGE was founded in 1965 by Sara Miller McCune to support the dissemination of usable knowledge by publishing innovative and high-quality research and teaching content. Today, we publish more than 750 journals, including those of more than 300 learned societies, more than 800 new books per year, and a growing range of library products including archives, data, case studies, reports, conference highlights, and video. SAGE remains majority-owned by our founder, and after Sara's lifetime will become owned by a charitable trust that secures our continued independence.

Los Angeles | London | Washington DC | New Delhi | Singapore

Social Work
Practice
Placements
Critical and Reflective Approaches

Sue Jones

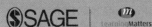

Los Angeles | London | New Delhi
Singapore | Washington DC

Series Editors:
Jonathan Parker and Greta Bradley

Learning Matters
An imprint of SAGE Publications Ltd
1 Oliver's Yard
55 City Road
London EC1Y 1SP

SAGE Publications Inc.
2455 Teller Road
Thousand Oaks, California 91320

SAGE Publications India Pvt Ltd
B 1/I 1 Mohan Cooperative Industrial Area
Mathura Road
New Delhi 110 044

SAGE Publications Asia-Pacific Pte Ltd
3 Church Street
#10-04 Samsung Hub
Singapore 049483

Editor: Kate Wharton
Development editor: Lauren Simpson
Production controller: Chris Marke
Project management: Swales & Willis Ltd,
    Exeter, Devon
Marketing manager: Tamara Navaratnam
Cover design: Wendy Scott
Typeset by: C&M Digitals (P) Ltd, Chennai, India
Printed by: Henry Ling Limited at
The Dorset Press, Dorchester, DT1 1HD

Library of Congress Control Number: 2014949772

British Library Cataloguing in Publication Data

A catalogue record for this book is available from the
British Library

ISBN 978-1-4739-0223-7
ISBN 978-1-4739-0224-4 (pbk)

At SAGE we take sustainability seriously. Most of our products are printed in the UK using FSC papers and boards.
When we print overseas we ensure sustainable papers are used as measured by the Egmont grading system.
We undertake an annual audit to monitor our sustainability.

Contents

• Using theory and critical thinking in your placement practice • Theories to help us understand the individual or situation • Methods • Strategies • Frameworks • Models • Deepening critical reflection • Developing learning opportunities to support your critical development • Creating your own critical learning questions while in placement

About the author

Sue Jones holds academic and professional qualifications in social work, teaching and sign language. She uses her many years of teaching experience in the UK and Eastern Europe and her numerous contacts with practice agencies over 25 years to inform her understanding of student learning needs in practice. She currently teaches, tutors and assesses on the BA and Master's social work courses at Manchester Metropolitan University. Sue is the English editor of the Lithuanian Journal *Special Education* published by Siauliai University and has received their Gold Award in recognition of outstanding service collaboration. Her first book *Critical Learning for Social Work Students* (2nd edition published in 2013 by Sage) serves as a foundation to academic learning and preface to this text.

Series editor's preface

The notion that social work practice placements represent those elements of qualifying education that people most remember has been often repeated, but it is nonetheless true for many social workers. In the US, the professional body called the Council on Social Work Education (CSWE) recognized explicitly the importance of the practice placement referring to it as social work's 'signature pedagogy', and in the UK we have embedded placements at the heart of our professional education for students qualifying in social work.

As well as being something that individual students and later qualified practitioners appreciate and remember, it is however the placement that has been the subject of tense and protracted political wrangling. This is something that has moulded and forged our current approaches in the UK, and something that permeates the negotiations and partnership agreements distilled between social work agencies and universities. It is in this political context that Sue Jones offers her valuable perspectives on social work placements. Whilst she writes specifically for the English context, this is valuable and translates across the UK, and indeed adds to the growing lexicon of work relating to practice placements across the world. The general and the specific sit together as we interpret the human condition in context. This book makes an important contribution to assisting social work students to unravel these complexities.

In this important book, Sue Jones adds a deeper critical perspective, something that is much needed since the evidence-base for the value of placements is still nascent. She builds on her earlier work encouraging students to adopt a critical and reflective understanding and this book will stand students in good stead as they begin their journeys into the complex and contorted landscapes of social work.

Jonathan Parker

Director, Centre of Social Work, Sociology & Social Policy, School of Health & Social Care, Bournemouth University

Acknowledgements

I continue to give my thanks to all past and current Bachelor and Master of Arts students at Manchester Metropolitan University who continue to inspire me with their thirst for learning. You are a credit to the social work profession.

To colleagues in the learning and teaching fields from whom critical debate has both urged me onwards and caused me to stop and reflect. Also to Sage publishers, and specifically Luke Block, Lauren Simpson and Kate Wharton, for their support.

Not least to my family: Hollin for your technical expertise; Carrick for your thoughtful conversations and to David for your initial proofreading.

Introduction

This book follows on from, and builds upon, *Critical Learning for Social Work Students* by the same author. Although it is written primarily for social work students undertaking practice placements, like the first book, the essential nature of the contents are equally applicable to students from other disciplines completing a practice placement in order to qualify in their vocational field. As adult learners we find the most effective and appropriate way to learn is through action rather than being told how to do something. We have a tendency towards applying our experience, skill and knowledge in action. Yet the act of learning how to do social work is highly complex and mired with numerous pitfalls and challenges. In working through the material and exercises in this book you will be exposed to these dilemmas and tensions, and hopefully begin to develop your own informed interpretations of social work in practice during your placements and beyond.

Recently, the professional standards for social workers have changed and, following the disbanding of the General Social Care Council (GSCC), were incorporated into the Health and Care Professions Council (HCPC). You can find the new standards at **www.hpc-uk.org**. In addition to evidencing your ability against these standards you will also have undertaken a course of education that is approved and monitored by the Quality Assurance Agency (QAA) for Higher Education. You will find statements from these two organisations at the beginning of each chapter relating to the standards to be covered. In line with changes in social work education, following recent serious case reviews (SCRs) and, significantly, the case of Peter Connelly, the training and development of your practice educators has also been redefined. These come under the remit of The College of Social Work (TCSW) and are known as Practice Educator Professional Standards (PEPS). By October 2015, all practice educators must be registered social workers with the HCPC. Some practice educators might choose to undertake stage one of this registration only and this will entitle them to supervise the first placement, but not the final one leading to qualification. Those practice educators having stage two registration can supervise up to and including the final placement and qualification recommendation report. It is important to understand these requirements of you and your practice educator as mechanisms to monitor the quality of provision and your capability to practise in the shifting and contested field that is social work. Although such scrutiny might feel overbearing at times, it will ensure that you enter the profession equipped with the professional armour to undertake the work and to represent the profession appropriately against media hyperbole and public disapproval. More importantly, along with revised systems, as proposed by Munro (2011) and the Hammersmith system (in Munro 2011), by reducing response and action times so that children do not die and the need for SCRs lessens, we may counter the charges that social workers spend too much time on their computers.

In a recent report entitled *Frontline* commissioned by the Institute for Public Policy Research (IPPR), employers of social workers were consulted and one director of children's services said that while the application rates for vacancies was high, the quality of applicants was not guaranteed. Employers are looking for very highly skilled and resilient practitioners who have the potential to develop as leaders in their field. They want to retain staff in frontline posts while also developing them as middle and senior leaders with expertise in their field. This is laudable, as good practitioners often wish to retain their practitioner status while, at the same time, developing their interests in, perhaps, action research, specialisms and workforce development. For this reason this book will encourage you to look beyond Newly Qualified Social Worker (NQSW) status towards your Assessed and Supported Year in Employment (ASYE).

In order to 'raise the game' in social work, to raise the quality of your work rather than being content to merely meet the minimum requirements, I propose that you should begin the journey of recognising yourself as a virtuous social worker. By that I mean that you should abide by a highly moral code so that your practice is at all times exemplary, whether or not you are under scrutiny. There are many excellent texts that will guide you in the practical elements of preparation for your placement. In this text I focus more on the virtuous aspects of your practice especially in Chapter 1, so that you can apply this learning to the rest of the book. In *Critical Learning for Social Work Students* you were guided through various learning tools and exercises. You should now be using these naturally in your academic learning and perhaps some of you have been using the later chapters in your placements. However, in this book you will have opportunities to challenge some of that theoretical learning, to see how it actually works in practice where agency cultures impinge on your values, ethics and practice and where your sense of self is challenged by less-than-optimum conditions in which to fulfil your stated quest of helping others when you were first interviewed for your course.

For these reasons, Chapter 1 begins with an examination of how you might prepare yourself for going on placement. In this chapter you will begin to appreciate the anticipatory, contemplative and accountable nature of work while in placement. You will begin to develop the ability to use deep and strategic levels of thinking in practice and to develop the ability to evidence critical practice that demonstrates engagement. At the end of the chapter you will be examining how this impacts on your ability to manage personal, professional and university life.

Chapter 2 takes you into the world of organisational considerations. Here you will look at a variety of organisational cultures and practices; you will be guided through a variety of documentation formats used by agencies and invited to offer a critique of these. As a considerable proportion of social work practice involves working with other professions, you will be guided to appreciate the need for, and seek information through, a range of multi-professional and collaborative activities. This leads on to a consideration of the use of power, both in a multi-disciplinary and your own agency context.

Chapter 3 moves into embedding critical placement learning through having an appreciation of your own learning style and knowing how to create your own fertile learning environment while in placement. In doing this, you will be applying and critically evaluating theories used in social work to the placement environment and interpreting learning opportunities using a strengths-based approach. In conclusion, the chapter moves towards working with the reality of placement and practice in that situations will present themselves that are far from perfect. You will be using your own experiences to recognise, and refer on appropriately, behaviours that are unprofessional.

Chapter 4 will prepare you for using supervision and practice observations through analysing and critiquing the organisational aspects and documentation of the supervisory and tutor relationships. In order that you should be able to engage in deep-level thinking and make maximum use of this time your preparation should demonstrate how you are critically evaluating the complexity of what you do in practice. This means valuing the learning to be gleaned from experiences that challenge you and those that affirm your abilities. Although part of the supervisory relationship is to impart what you have done, this is essentially a descriptive activity that has minimal effect as a driver for deep learning. Therefore, within this chapter you will be encouraged to model your conversations on the work of Fook. This philosophical approach, tempered with human rights and responsibility, will enable you to adequately debate and act upon areas of risk, rights and power relevant to practice. Having confidence in your reflections will give you the skills to receive, and act positively on, feedback from practice and assessments of practice.

Chapter 5 deals with the completion of the portfolio and, although it appears towards the end of the book, you must begin to gather evidence from the very beginning of placement. Selecting appropriate elements of practice with which to evidence the Professional Capabilities Framework (PCF) domain standards and the HCPC ethics and codes for social work students is a perpetual exercise. You will be jettisoning early examples for more complex and critical work as you move through the placement. Chapter 5 will show you how to use reflective and reflexive language in order to demonstrate deep-learning language skills. Elements of confidentiality and anonymity will be opened up and broadened to a range of stakeholders. You will be shown opportunities where you might exemplify your skills of analysis and evaluation in synthesising theory and practice in succinct ways.

Chapter 6 opens up the beginning of your career trajectory, from your NQSW status through your first ASYE, considering your employment opportunities and the requirements of employers to make appropriate support available. Emphasis is given to your consolidation of reflective and critical attributes that you will have developed using this book and how these should be progressed through a portfolio method during your ASYE and forthcoming continuing professional development (CPD).

As expected of the Transforming Social Work Practice series, this book is highly interactive in that there are case studies, activities, reflection points and commentary notes, as well as knowledge-based learning, templates and diagrams. The chapters are not necessarily contingent upon each other in a linear style so you do not need to follow them in the order they are presented. You may dip into the book according to your learning needs as they arise. You might find certain aspects that stimulate you to find out more and to aid you with this there are tips for texts and websites at the end of each chapter. Essentially the book is your tool, but as with most tools you need several to do the job. Be curious in your quest for knowledge and set yourself questions that you might not be able to answer immediately. Seek out other, more specific texts about, for example, theory, philosophy, government guidance or SCRs and take responsibility for what and how you learn.

Finally, I want to re-emphasise the nature of what it means to be 'critical' by high-lighting the following nine areas of critical learning within your practice.

What is 'critical'?

In professional life, and especially where working directly with others, including users of social care services, their carers, colleagues and other professionals, you will be developing a sensitivity to appreciate positions of which you have no experience.

You will need to be careful that you *do not* . . .

- unintentionally misuse your power;
- misunderstand key issues of discrimination and oppression;
- fail to recognise significant events;
- minimise the need to take action.

and that you *do* . . .

- step back and reflect on your practice and that of others;
- recognise the potential for discrimination and oppression;
- consider a wide range of influential factors;
- take informed action where there is actual or potential risk.

In learning how to *do* these last four you will be developing your ability to:

Critique: see the nuances as well as the obvious in what you read and hear. This is not like 'criticism' where there is a tendency to see only the negative aspects. A critique would offer a balanced view of all aspects.

Analyse: be discerning about how you gather information and recognise the significance of its structure and constituent parts. This means not only choosing those aspects of an issue that agree with what you think but also those that are contrary to your beliefs.

Evaluate: judge the quality and importance or value of something. This is about how you are able to weigh up what significance something would have to your argument.

Synthesise: fuse different ideas together to create a new 'whole'. This is how you are able to make connections between ideas with the result that you create new perspectives, usually those with more complexity than previously imagined.

It involves deductive and inductive reasoning, and often the resolution of conflict created by opposing positions or arguments.

Reframe: create a new position for an argument. This is how you see that critical learning has taken place because you are able to let go of previously held views by replacing them with your new understandings.

And to deal with:

Dilemmas and tensions: the deep thinking needed for critical engagement will cause you to continue to question yourself, even when the answer appears to be easy. You will become aware that surface-level thinking leads to inadequate understanding and creates simplistic solutions.

Unknowing: the realisation that in any area you cannot have all the information or know the absolute truth. Usually you will be working with nuances, alternative perspectives to your own and any decisions you make can only be tentative, 'good enough' in the moment and must be open to rethinking.

Uncertainty: in order to flourish, professionals need to be able to cope with self-doubt. You are a human being and humans make mistakes. Use these occasions for growth, take from them learning experiences and recognise them as integral to the experience of working with the uniqueness of the human condition in an ever-changing environment.

Emotional confusion: professional life is peppered with elation and despair. One day it is the best thing in the world, the next it can be the worst and on other days it can be anywhere in between, from run-of-the-mill to exhilarating. Learning how to deal with this rollercoaster is fundamental to your own well-being and you will do well to draw around you a support network with which to share, commiserate and advise on your practice.

In summary, these nine areas form the constituent parts of the *critical* when attached to questioning, reading, writing, reasoning, thinking and to practice, analysis, evaluation and synthesis. Another way to understand what *critical* elements are is that they are those things that cause you to be restless and unsatisfied when you feel you have not fully explored or 'bottomed' all aspects of something. It is rather like having a small insect that keeps trying to bite you even though you keep wafting it away. Give the insect some thought and you might trap it in a box and put it outside, remove yourself from the room, put up a fly trap or spray yourself with fly repellent. When you next encounter such a fly you will know how to deal with it effectively! So it is with the *critical* fly: meet it head on and it will become increasingly easier and effective to use.

Placement structure and purpose

By the time you begin to think about your practice placements you might be at one of three stages in your course. Some programmes have a short, 30-day placement in the first year of the course with the remaining 170 days spread out over the second and third years, typically with 70 days in year two and 100 days in year three, while others have an equal 100 days in both the second and third years. (Postgraduate students do their placements over the two years of their course.) Generally, the total number of days in your placements will be 200, although there are some variations to this in Northern Ireland where the requirement is for 185 in total. Whatever stage you are at, you are likely to be apprehensive about your forthcoming placement. Even though you might have successfully undertaken one or two placements already, there is always the anticipation of a new venue, practice educator, staff group, agency policy and practice because your course placement managers will always try to give you alternative experiences. Indeed, as required by the Department of Health:

> Each student must have experience in at least two practice settings, and of 'statutory social work tasks involving legal interventions'. They must also provide services to 'at least two user groups (for example, child care and mental health)'.

(Carson, 2010)

Although it is a requirement that social work students are assessed on placement, you need not think that you will be alone in this as, according to Corinne May-Chahal, co-chair of TCSW, placements are a three-way partnership between the student, the organisation, and the college or university.

> Practice assessors supervise and mentor students, and in doing so they are contributing to their own professional development. University tutors have ongoing relationships with placement providers and can feed in new learning through placement visits, information sharing and training days. Employers also have the chance to get to know students and consider their potential as future employees. In cases where the employer sponsors an employee to train as a social worker, placements enable the retention of good staff by offering a career development opportunity. Service users can often benefit from an organisation that provides placements, because their student social worker will have smaller caseloads and more time to dedicate to learning new ways of working.

(May-Chahal, 2010)

Although you will have had considerable opportunities for academic learning in your university programme, in applied professional courses such as social work you must also be assessed in practice. Imagine being operated on by a doctor who has only learnt how to do the operation by reading about it! Also, you are not practising in isolation; in addition to your practice educator, or practice supervisor (if you have an off-site practice educator) you also have access to the resources of the team, the agency as a whole and to the allied professionals with whom you will come into contact as a result of multi-agency working. Some agencies also have student support groups where you will be able to mix with other students on social work and allied professional courses, and one large advantage is that you might be able to take advantage of their in-house training opportunities. These can sometimes boost your curriculum vitae when applying for work.

How will this book support me while on placement?

In this book, you will find examples that will expose dilemmas and tensions, conflict and critique that will enable you to examine situations you are likely to come across. There are sample pro-formas and policy guidance that you can use to critique the purpose of service provision. You will approach your learning using the binary of a philosophical approach that is based on the nature of the virtuous social worker juxtaposed with the discourse of fiscal restraint, rights/responsibility-based provision and within the creativity and compromise of real practice.

Therefore, this book will encourage you to look towards your ASYE and, while it is mandatory that you provide evidence that you are able to practise to set standards, it is important that you are not constrained by them. This is especially true of the final placement leading to your qualification status.

Chapter 1

Preparation for your social work placement

This chapter will help you to develop the following capabilities, to the appropriate level, from the Professional Capabilities Framework:

- *Professionalism*: Demonstrate ability to learn, using a range of approaches.
- *Critical reflection and analysis*: Understand the role of reflective practice and demonstrate basic skills of reflection. Understand the need to construct hypotheses in social work practice.

It will also introduce you to the following standards as set out in the 2008 Social Work Subject Benchmark Statement:

4.2   At Honours level, the study of social work involves the integrated study of subject-specific knowledge, skills and values and the critical application of research knowledge from the social and human sciences, and from social work to inform understanding and to underpin action, reflection and evaluation . . . and to foster this integration of contextual, analytic, critical explanatory and practical understanding.

4.4   Honours graduates in social work should be equipped to both understand and work within a context of contested debate about nature, scope and purpose and be enabled to analyse, adapt to, manage and eventually to lead the processes of change.

6.2   The learning process in social work as expressed in awareness raising, skills and knowledge acquisition, conceptual understanding, practice skills and experience and reflection on performance.

Introduction

The focus of this chapter will be for you to reposition yourself within the domain of placement learning. I invite the term 'reposition' because so far on your course you will have been coming to terms with who you are within the context of academic life as an undergraduate or postgraduate student. Working through this chapter will help to prepare you to demonstrate a high level of professionalism through knowing what to expect from the placement. This will include the ability to situate your experiences within placement expectations and to articulate these effectively using your course documentation. You might think about how to express your experience as a carer. What skills and knowledge do you have that would transfer over to the placement? If you have only worked in a non-statutory organisation how might you articulate your roles and tasks for a potential statutory placement? Perhaps you would use organisational rather than descriptive terms. So if you worked on an advice line for the Samaritans you might express this as having a calm and resourceful manner, able to deal with crisis situations and having good communication skills. Through an understanding of how decisions are made as to the allocation of a placement within an agency you will appreciate that there are different ways to express your knowledge, experience, aspirations and qualifications on the placement application form.

For example, your placement request form will be sent via the university placement team to an agency representative who will then select a staff member to be your potential practice educator. They might reject your request if they feel they cannot provide you with an appropriate learning opportunity. The person who eventually makes a judgement about whether there is a 'fit' between your requirements and their offer is wholly reliant on what they read on your form. There is a skill in writing the request form that is broad enough to encompass various fields of practice and demonstrates a depth to your experience and aspirations.

Also, it is vital that you demonstrate your openness to engage with learning, and to welcome challenge and set out what you judge your learning needs to be. An example of a completed placement request form is given in this chapter. Throughout the chapter you will begin to recognise social work as a considered and carefully expressed enterprise where reflective and critical thinking is paramount. Some dilemmas will be posed for you where you have to work with situations that are not of your choosing yet provide opportunities of breadth and depth that will lead you to a wealth of career trajectories as yet unconsidered.

By the end of this chapter you will be able to:

- demonstrate an ability to manage personal, professional and university life while successfully completing the placement;

- prepare for your practice placement using an appreciation of the necessary knowledge, skills and aptitudes;

- recognise and evidence your existing abilities and knowledge through a contemplative approach that enables you to express these formally to the placement providers;

- anticipate the essential factors surrounding the placement experience and their place in your own professional behaviours.

The placement structure

The College of Social Work (TCSW) has set down guidance to universities and employers on the expectations of readiness for practice in social work students who are preparing to undertake practice placements in service provider agencies. The structure of these is as follows:

Undergraduate programmes

- *Year One*: 30 days of developing skills for practice.

- *Year Two*: 70 days of formal practice, practice educator supervision and assessment, followed by the student submission of a portfolio of evidence to the Practice Assessment Board.

- *Year Three*: 100 days of formal practice to include practice knowledge of statutory requirements, practice educator supervision and assessment, followed by the student submission of a portfolio of evidence to the Practice Assessment Board. Placement two should offer learning experiences with a different service user group from placement one.

Postgraduate programmes

- *Year One*: 100 days of formal practice, practice educator supervision and assessment, followed by the student submission of a portfolio of evidence to the Practice Assessment Board.

- *Year Two*: 100 days of formal practice to include practice knowledge of statutory requirements, practice educator supervision and assessment followed by the student submission of a portfolio of evidence to the Practice Assessment Board. Placement two should offer learning experiences with a different service user group from placement one.

In both routes the Professional Capabilities Framework (PCF) will apply throughout and your course might decide to separate them so that the complexity is heightened as you progress through the programme. The portfolio will demonstrate a standard of competence that must be clearly evidenced in practice. This includes the ability to think critically, reflect, create personal learning opportunities, work individually and with a team and manage the tensions and dilemmas of the work created by contentious situations in which there is often no clear resolution. The PCF is included as Appendix 1 of this book for your information. Alternatively, it can be accessed at **www.tcsw.org.uk** along with a wealth of information relating to social work placements. As the framework for learning also includes the Higher Education Subject Benchmarks for Social Work, these can be accessed online at **www.qaa.ac.uk**.

Reflecting on skills for placement

While working in the placement agencies you will also be attending university, either one or two days a week, maybe taking a specialist unit or returning for contact days once every two months or so. The level of contact differs with each programme. How might this shifting attendance pattern affect you?

---

*ACTIVITY **1.1***

Preparing for placement: the reality of practice

What questions might arise for you in meeting the needs of the programme structure once you are on placement? Read the following then review alongside the Comment section.

> *Shamira had managed to get her head around what social work was about after the first few terms at university – at least theoretically. She now knew it was about*

Continued

---

social change, risk and protection, control and empowerment. She had shadowed a social worker in a child protection team and in her reflective report about this had confessed to feeling overwhelmed. She had looked at her own family, her own children and the support she both received and gave and could not reconcile this with the treatment that the children in the placement had received from their parents. She thought them irresponsible – taking drugs and drinking, not clean-ing the house or making sure that the children got to school. Shamira had now found that her first placement was in a child protection team at some distance from her home. She was worried about compromising the care of her own chil-dren as she would need to leave them with a childminder before and after school. She also felt her feelings would compromise whether she would be able to help these families if she were their social worker. She didn't want to mention this to her tutor or lecturers as they might think her unsuitable to continue on the course but she made a note to speak to some of the other students at the callback day.

COMMENT

Shamira struggled with the reality of social work practice. She had felt competent in the knowledge from her academic learning and although she had researched the law rele-vant to her practice she felt her own value base was intervening and preventing her from engaging with the family. She was anxious because she felt it necessary to hide her feel-ings from the university and placement staff. She genuinely wanted to help the family but seemed unable to resolve her difficulties in order to act as an advocate on their behalf. No matter how much she delved into her capacities for thinking through these things she felt insincere and always returned in a cyclical manner to her original unhelpful thoughts. In effect, she was unable to act as an independent thinker because her personal views were interfering with her professional self. One might say there was too much 'noise' from her private entity that was not being resolved in order to deal with her professional persona. Shamira needed to develop her skills in deep reflection, linking with socio-psychological theories and situating herself within a set of professional ideas that would act as a catalyst to both reflexive and critical positioning.

In dealing with this dilemma Shamira might apply the work of Jung (1989) and of Bourdieu et al. (1992). Jung uses the concept of 'individuation' to describe how we apply our sense of who we are (the self) to fulfil our potential for all that we can be. In this way, Shamira recognises the dilemmas she faces. There is a need to integrate the two distinct parts of her psyche; the personal versus the professional self applied to what she knows must consti-tute her values, beliefs and behaviours in social work practice. In a similar vein, Bourdieu speaks of our 'habitus' in recognising that our whole personality is contributed to by our lifelong experiences and how these have been imbibed to form our aptitudes and abilities in our interpretation of the world over a period of time. This process continues throughout

Continued

life causing us to constantly reflect on, and revise, our perceptions of how we act in the world. Here Shamira recognises the impact of her life so far on her ability to act in certain ways and to question the rightness of these ways. These two approaches cause her to accept the dissonance that might exist once she experiences the practice of social work. In reasoning in this way, she will see the need to take her feelings to supervision as a professional activity and not as a failure to be thinking the 'right' thoughts.

It is through the questioning, relinquishing or embedding of our psychological makeup as social workers that we develop the emotional resilience needed to undertake the social work role.

Developing your resilience while on placement

Most social work students have embarked on their careers wanting to help others and it comes as a shock that some of the work may involve working with people who are involuntary service users and unlikeable. It is therefore vital that you prepare your personal life to run as smoothly as possible and know how to manage difficulties that will invariably arise while you are on placement. Posing yourself some questions to deal with your feelings will help you to see more clearly through the fog of your emotions. Here are some to help you.

1. *What do I need to do to ensure that my children and I are comfortable with the arrangements for childcare before and after school? How can I manage the financial implications of this?* It is essential that your mind is free to concentrate on your placement, and worrying about family matters will mean that you are not engaging well with service users.

2. *What would be the implications of discussing my feelings about placement with my tutor?* The call back days or unit teaching days give you some grounding back to the university and your tutors. Any problems on the placement should first be expressed to your practice educator, and on-site supervisor if you have an off-site practice educator. However, tutors are happy to listen to your concerns and suggest some strategies for resolution. Indeed, the raising of such issues is considered good practice. You can also see your student group as a resource and choose to discuss your fears with a critical friend.

3. *How will I manage the traffic at such busy times and over such a long distance?* This is a question to address at the pre-placement meeting as agencies are generally very flexible, allowing the required seven hours a day to be managed outside traffic pressure times.

4. *How will I hand in my assignments while on placement as I will not be able to get to university?* It might be possible to ask a fellow student who is near to

your university to do this for you, or you can ask about postal arrangements. Generally, it is acceptable to post work in if the date of postage shown on the package corresponds to the hand-in date. Increasingly universities are moving to online submissions.

5. *Placement is like a full-time job so how will I manage to complete my assignments at the same time?* Vocational courses have to combine academic and practice work according to their professional bodies, in this case the HCPC. This is stated on all documentation relating to social work programmes. Once qualified, you will be required to continue your professional development, so working and learning need to be embedded as a habit to continue throughout your professional life. This is no different from doctors, teachers, solicitors, etc.

Forward thinking in ways such as these will enable you to develop a contemplative approach where you develop skills to anticipate potential difficulties and pleasures in your work. It will also evidence your accountability, when questioned, about any actions you choose to take or withhold.

Placement knowledge and skills

The selection process to allow you to gain entry to the course will have begun to assess your knowledge and skills according to the PCF. These are as follows:

> . . . by the point of entry to social work qualifying programmes, prospective students/candidates should demonstrate awareness of the social context for social work practice, awareness of self, ability to develop rapport and potential to develop relevant knowledge, skills and values through professional train-ing. They will have as the minimum academic thresholds, spoken and written English, maths and IT. The selection process will generally be expected to have an individual interview, a written test and wherever possible, group activi-ties. In addition to academic staff, employers and service users and carers are involved in the selection processes.

(Author's note: Master's students will have a relevant degree.)

Full details of criteria and processes can be found at: **www.tcsw.org.uk** in the TCSW Final HEI Toolkit.

The 30 day practice skills development will engage you in learning about what social work is, how your values and beliefs impact on the work and how you will recognise and deal with the tensions and dilemmas you will encounter. You will learn about the placement-finding process, discussed later in this chapter, and the social work pro-cesses used in agencies. This might involve you in shadowing a qualified social worker and the completion of a reflective commentary on your learning. Other aspects of the pre-placement period might include how to use supervision, how to critically reflect on learning about topics such as the identification, analysis and management of risk, statements of fact and opinion, recording systems, how to create and use a learning log, how to use theory in creating assessments and how to adapt communication skills in a variety of situations. TCSW states that some of the 30 days may be used to work on higher-level skills between the first and second placements. This would be a useful engagement where students might share the agenda by highlighting what areas they had difficulty with while in the first practice placement and academics could introduce ideas of the reflexive and virtuous social worker.

ACTIVITY *1.2*

Read this definition of social work from the International Federation of Social Work:

The social work profession **promotes social change, problem solving in human relationships and the empowerment and liberation of people to enhance well-being.** Utilising **theories of human behaviour and social systems, social work intervenes at the points where people interact with their environments.** Principles **of human rights and social justice are fundamental to social work.**

(www.ifsw.org; author's emphasis)

Take each of the terms emphasised above and jot down how you think the knowledge and skills might be practised in response to contemporary social work. So, for example, one clear area of change would be in the law. What are the current laws that you think might be quoted in order to cope with social change? Some might be needed to protect vulnerable people in response to what we know about abuse. Some might be in the merging of services in order to make access to them seamless and others to implement the criteria for professional training, for example, in social work and nursing.

COMMENT

Have you ever tried to write a statement, for example: 'What is motherhood'? If you did, you would quickly realise that any attempt at such a definition is rooted in history, culture, chronology, class, age, ability, gender and, not least, experience. Also, these constituents are influenced by our own lifelong experiences, as Pierre Bourdieu (Jenkins, 1982) would say our 'habitus' and, as Daniel Goleman (1998) might interject, as being due to our 'emotional intelligence'. (See Jones (2013) for further clarification of these ideas.) It follows, then, that academic attempts to define social work are dependent on time and place and are shifting and contested. The knowledge and skills needed follow similar pathways of change within what we understand as 'empowerment', human rights and social justice. In what ways are we seeking to promote social change and why? How are the problems we seek to solve similar or different to those in previous times? What has been the impact of change in social behaviour and social systems? One might quote the changing discourses on motherhood, adoption, gay rights, child abuse and the use of computers in the management of risk and information sharing to see how year-by-year the knowledge and skills required to practise social work are adapting.

What do you understand by the IFSW definition? The first topic in the definition is about 'social change'. We often want service users to change but is this really what social work

Continued

is about? Could the statement be referring to society changing to become more equitable by giving vulnerable people more support in education or employment?

How is it possible to solve the problems in human relationships and promote empower-ment when we live in a divided society where some communities see social resourcing as the norm and where generations of claimants have never worked? Should the statement regarding where individuals interact with the environment really read: 'Where the envi-ronment interacts with individuals?' When do personal problems become public concerns causing the state to intervene?

Principles of human rights and social justice are laudable, but for whom? Who are those for whom such considerations are disallowed? Child murderers and paedophiles, of course, you might say, but what about older and disabled people for whom the social resourcing for an additional bedroom has recently been deemed unacceptable?

Has it become possible for the rule on social resourcing to become the victim of gov-ernment rationalisation, at any cost? If so, then we are looking at a society that readily manipulates support for the vulnerable to reflect the resourcing available. This will be the reality of your placement experience, despite the values and beliefs of the agency, you or your work colleagues.

More about skills

In your academic work you will have become familiar with the skills associated with practice and these will include:

(a) skills used in the application of social work theory, e.g. crisis intervention, systems and network, solution focused, task centred, psychodynamic;

(b) skills used in communication, e.g. non-verbal, use of eye contact, non-judgemental, acceptance, self-determination, unconditional positive regard;

(c) skills in researching and compiling written material, following course rules and regulational procedures and meeting deadlines;

(d) skills of reflection, critical analysis and evaluation in your assignments;

(e) skills in self-awareness, e.g. interacting with peers, redefining/asserting your values and beliefs, analysing dilemmas and tensions.

The above skills will all be taken with you into practice. There is fundamentally no separation between the skills learned in university and those applied in practice. Although students often think that the 'real element' of their course is practice, this cannot be undertaken without recourse to the development of a strong foundation from which to ground your continuing professional development. Think of your expe-rience as the archaeology that has informed who you are. Think of your foundations as academic learning and the placement experience as the scaffolding or architecture for your current and future professional development. This will form your lifelong learning journey through social work practice, as to practise is to learn.

In applying the ideas of an archaeology and architecture to your placement you will have to think about how you will develop the list above – (a) to (e) – in the fulfilment of practice skills. For example taking (a), you will need to find out what theory(ies) are used in the placement. What are the skill sets associated with their application? Is there a culture of one particular theory and why? What are the methods used to apply, evaluate and monitor the work? Do you think a more appropriate theory could be used and why? Would the agency be open to adopt different approaches? Are there powerful personnel who hold onto these methods and resist change? Is theory invisible but practice based on a pragmatic and eclectic approach with a 'well it is what we always do' approach? How might you challenge this with your practice educator?

ACTIVITY *1.3*

Skills in practice

Taking (b) to (e) inclusively from the list above, translate how you might prepare for their adaptation into practice.

COMMENT

This activity mirrors the work that you will do in your reflective practice journals while on placement. A quote from a participant in action research carried out in Cork stated that this sort of activity is as follows:

> . . . a tool to use to try to be more present to yourself in every way – how you are impacted by social work interaction, how the client is impacted. A set of skills which equips you, provokes you, keeps you interested, freshens questions I can ask myself.

> *(Dempsey et al., 2008)*

So, in preparing for your placement you will be:

(b) researching the skills used in communication, looking at cultural differences, learning how to pick up on non-verbal clues, dealing with any prejudices you have, developing your empathy and learning how to elicit the perspectives of disadvantaged others;

(c) developing your skills in researching and compiling written material, dealing with any difficulties you have in writing formal reports, developing an appropriate writing style for various purposes, assessing the impact of the agency culture, e.g. power dynamics, managerialism, following agency policy and procedures and challenging these appropriately where necessary, meeting deadlines, responding to hierarchical change and working with management information systems;

Continued

COMMENT *continued*

(d) using skills of reflection, reflexive and critical analysis and evaluation on your practice using adult learning principles, for example, through the ability to develop a personal learning style where you apply a retrospective (reflective), action-orientated (reflexive) and structural (critical) understanding of your practice;

(e) using skills in self-awareness, e.g. interacting with peers, redefining/asserting your values and beliefs, analysing dilemmas and tensions, representing your agency appropriately, driving your learning forward in the supervisory relationship, taking ownership of your own development and seeking learning opportunities.

In developing these skills you will access tools that are relevant to you but, additionally, you will be exploring the broader elements of practice linked to criticality. These are applied to all your work and constitute the notion of professionalism in social work. I refer here to the aptitudes of trust, confidence and mindfulness and to the use of reasoning skills and the introduction of ideas such as spirituality, power, oppression and discrimination. I also refer to the skills of accountability, not only in the limited sense of the agency, but to ideas of national and global poverty, abuse, and governmental manipulation through discourse and social constructionism.

These may seem such big ideas that they are impossible for you to hold in your head but if you are working within social work you do not need to go far before you are aware of their impact on your practice and, therefore, on the skills you will need to develop as a consummate professional.

Placement aims

Let us turn now to look at how some writers have encapsulated the aims of the 70-day placement.

The first (70-day) practice placement will engage students with the four main aims in the practice curriculum as follows:

- *to develop core knowledge and skills;*
- *to foster a critically reflective approach to practice;*
- *to develop a self-responsibility for learning;*
- *to identify learning needs and to plan how these can be met.*

(Parker, 2010, p68)

Braye and Preston-Shoot state the four aims of the placement as:

- *awareness raising, skills and knowledge acquisition;*
- *conceptual understanding;*
- *practice skills and experience;*
- *reflection on performance.*

(Braye and Preston-Shoot, 2008)

In preparing for your first placement you must begin to develop and build on your skills in critical thinking that allow you to stand back and contemplate a considered approach to the placement experience. It would be useful if you could pose some questions for yourself now.

REFLECTION POINT

Write at least three reflective questions that you might research before going to the pre-placement meeting. Then look at the list of questions below. You will see that some activities are simply satisfied with a definitive answer whereas others require a more critical approach.

In order to show that you have found out about the placement and are engaged with planning your learning you might need to carry out some research. Read any information you can about the placement, web pages, mission statements, details about service user groups and any evaluations of the service, government reports, SCIE best practice guidance, fair access to care, eligibility criteria, how to access an assessment and how to challenge it. You should also think about any applicable legislation, government policy documents and articles that challenge provision and read these before attending the pre-placement meeting. This will enable you to show that you already have skills and knowledge in certain areas as well as where your learning needs lie. You do not have to know about everything, of course, but being able to set your learning in the placement context, including academic learning from the university, will enable you to shine at the meeting.

Some practical questions you might like to ask at the pre-placement meeting might include:

- What is the dress code?

- What do I do if I am ill or late for an appointment?

- Is it possible to take holidays and whom should I inform?

- What time shall I come on the first day and where shall I report to?

- Is it possible to arrange the day so I can avoid the rush hour traffic?

- What do staff normally do for lunch?

- Do I have to bring my own cup or buy biscuits? (This might seem trivial but many a student has been embarrassed because the office culture was not explained to them!)

You should also be thinking about when the placement date will apply, the approximate dates of your mid- and end-placement meetings and the dates for submission of any assignments while on placement. Increasingly, the academic and practice fields of your learning are becoming more integrated and there are likely to be academic assignments that relate to your placement practice as well as placement-assessed assignments that must show integration of theoretical learning from the university units. Being prepared with these dates at the pre-placement meeting not only reduces the meeting time for busy practitioners, but demonstrates that you are already engaging with the duties of the placement.

There are nine competence descriptors in the PCF; eight of these sit comfortably with the first practice placement and being well-evidenced will allow you to progress to the final placement. These are Professionalism, Values and Ethics, Diversity, Justice, Knowledge, Judgement, Critical Reflection and Analysis, Contexts and Organisations. The ninth category of Professional Leadership may consider your undertaking a small piece of work that offers new learning to the agency or team. This can be accomplished by sharing some of the theories used in social work with the agency staff in order to improve practice. In some ways it could be considered as you giving something back to the agency as a thank you for sharing their expertise with you.

CASE STUDY 1.1

Read this example of how one student changed the focus of her placement agency's theoretical approach.

> *Ruth was working in a formal agency with children who were excluded from, or at risk of exclusion from school. Staff stated that they used 'child-centred theory' to engage the young people and their families in working towards remaining in, or reintegrating back into school.*

Ruth had been learning about systems theory at university and could see the relevance of it in her own life, how everything was connected and interlinked. She remembered how her own schoolwork had taken a dip when she became a carer for her mum and for a time she rebelled at school. Luckily, she had some good support from her friend's mum, her coach at athletics and the young carer's group she attended. In supervision with her practice educator, she explained that she would like to try using a different theory from the agency norm and she began to use network maps as part of a systemic approach to understanding the young people she was working with, and their families. The results were quite outstanding as she worked with some intransigent situations using visual methods to expose strengths and weaknesses, drivers and blockers in the young people's lives. Consequently the practice educator asked Ruth to hold some staff sessions to expose her achievements, and systems theory was adopted by all staff as a new methodology in the agency.

COMMENT

Ruth did not set herself up as an expert in systems theory but as someone prepared to take a risk with a different approach. It might not have worked and she was prepared to take the consequences, seeing it as a positive learning experience on her part. Her critical approach to practice did not criticise the agency's existing approach but sought

Continued

to complement it. She was sensitive to her position as a student and her colleagues' position as trained professionals. In effect Ruth used her emotional intelligence to collaborate, to focus on a service user orientation, spending time in developing others, by knowing how to cultivate opportunities, whom to work through and being politically aware of the culture of the organisational practices (see Goleman, 1998; Jones, 2013, chapter 5). 'We have always done it this way' does not mean it is effective. Ruth's empathy towards the young people and their families, and her belief that they could have a better service, plus her courage to effect change buoyed her professional confidence and the development of her skills.

RESEARCH SUMMARY

Emotional intelligence (EI) is one of the multiple intelligences we recognise as useful to social work alongside appreciative inquiry and the development of knowledge, skills, values and beliefs (see Jones, 2013, chapter 5 for references on EI and AI). One might say these are all intelligences in their own right as they imply a heightened ability for critical analysis and application in the betterment of life experiences.

In 2012 Richard Ingram wrote an article for the British Journal of Social Work in which he prefaced the centrality of EI and social work to the inclusion of service users. He went on to claim that EI not only integrated well with reflective and critical practice but that there were broader applications across the entire field of social work as a professional activity.

However, the notion of the development of resilience under stress and of supervision and safety was further raised by Ingram in 2013 when researching the reality of sharing emotional content in professional supervision. He found that, due to the pressure of managerial agendas that were being introduced to the supervisory relationship, social workers found that peer discussions better furthered the development of their emotional engagement with practice.

So while there is a clear and beneficial link between social work and EI, the embedding of such practice as a professional skill is rather covert due to the technical rationalism of management.

The final 100-day placement will offer opportunities for you to build on the skills and knowledge from placement one. You will be revisiting your existing levels of competence within the placement-finding process and developing the archaeology and the architecture of your profile to encompass the final placement objectives. This also means an integration of the code of practice for social work students and the development of a more critically reflexive style. You will demonstrate that you are able to critically reflect on practice and also see how action that emanates from your analysis leads to a synthesis of your learning within a professional context that encompasses world views and virtuous social work. More of this in Chapter 3.

According to TCSW, **the final 100-day placement** must prepare students for the statutory aspects of a social worker's role by offering them opportunities to demonstrate engagement with:

- *formal assessment processes (observation, gathering of information, analysis, reporting, use of evidence base, development of clear recommendations);*

- *application and understanding of legal frameworks relevant for social work practice (PCF 5, 8);*

- *organisational policies and decisions and their impact on service delivery to service users (PCF 8);*

- *the demands of a high-pressured environment, where time and competing interests have to be managed effectively (PCF 1);*

- *multi-agency working, including planning interventions with other agencies, and analysing and managing tensions (PCF 7, 8);*

- *presentation of outcomes of formal assessment processes, including analysis of risk/recommendations in line with organisational policy/procedure, e.g. at panels/meetings/courts (PCF 6, 7, 8);*

- *use of formal agency recording for assessment/risk.*

(www.tcsw.org.uk)

This does not indicate that you must have a statutory placement but that the activities undertaken in the placement must be commensurate with those undertaken within such agencies. Thus a local authority child protection department may devolve support to a family, who are close to meeting the criteria for the removal of children, to the voluntary sector, for example Sure Start or an equivalent. The latter would then present evidence, framed within the statutory requirements, to the local authority who would then take action dependent upon it.

ACTIVITY **1.4**

Mohan's placement was in a Sure Start programme where he ran small groups and undertook individual work with six families who had almost reached the threshold for the removal of their children under the 1989 Children Act. He had worked with the agency resources on parenting, risk identification, analysis and management and had used crisis intervention theory and systems analysis as his methodology. He had been scrupulous in documenting the extent to which the families' levels of engagement, progress and change were occurring and had used the agency's management information system (computer record system) to both document and share this within a multi-agency framework and timescale. Mohan contributed to the final report that his practice educator presented to the multi-disciplinary meeting to decide what action would be taken for each of the families. He had accessed resources in the team and been accountable for their use. He had

Continued

obtained further funding through diversity education in order to fund external events for the families to enable him to assess them in informal social settings, for example in their ability to manage their children appropriately in public situations. Although he was not allowed to present the case for removal at court he had attended the court proceedings and contributed a significant part to the report.

How do you think Mohan's placement met the criteria for 'statutory work'?

COMMENT

There are clear links that you can make to the TCSW list of areas from the PCF but try to look behind and beyond these in your analysis of statutory work. For example, what tensions and dilemmas might have been present in the work? Might the statutory authority have either urged or resisted the children being removed from their parents and what might have been their reasons for this? Might this have been influenced by resourcing, austerity cut-backs, lack of child care places with foster carers or residential homes, or in taking a risk-averse approach just in case anything should happen and the statutory authority be held responsible?

How do you think Mohan had to 'prepare a defence' for his recommendations? What aspects of legislation would he have had to use to underpin his legitimate use of power? What skills in assessment, observation, communication and recording might he have found useful? How could Mohan have used his emotional intelligence to be intuitive, contemplative or reflective? As he is working at the edge of social work, between care and control, with bureaucracy and user participation, with managerialism and individual professional judgement and artistry and regulation, how might he reconcile all these thoughts and actions to achieve a balanced and professional view capable of justification under scrutiny?

What, you say? How is it possible for each social worker to do all that while conforming to the paperwork? Always the paper work! You would be correct in assuming that nowadays the drive to systematise and regulate social work by desk-based administration is crowding out the original person-to-person engagement that social workers used to have with their service users. The fact is that contemporary social work, albeit a response to serious case reviews, austerity, changing demographics and governments, is rather like a juggling act.

But, I hear you say, I didn't want to join a circus! So what can offer you a place of solace where you can reconcile and justify your actions without the need to be a perfect social worker? How can you begin to accept that your work is performed within a contested and shifting theatre, and that it will ever be so? The answer is critical and reflexive learning, thinking and action. It is the armour with which you will bear the emotional content of your role.

Thinking about these issues in advance will prepare you to evidence statutory working whether you have a statutory placement or not and your university will have quality assured the placement to ensure the learning opportunities will give you opportunities to evidence such practice. Although not exclusively the province of the final placement, critical and reflexive thinking should be clearly embedded within your work at this level. This will enable you to go seamlessly into your ASYE and set up good habits for your continuing professional development trajectory.

Using a contemplative approach will help you to recognise and evidence your existing abilities in readiness for the placement request. The placement matching process will be

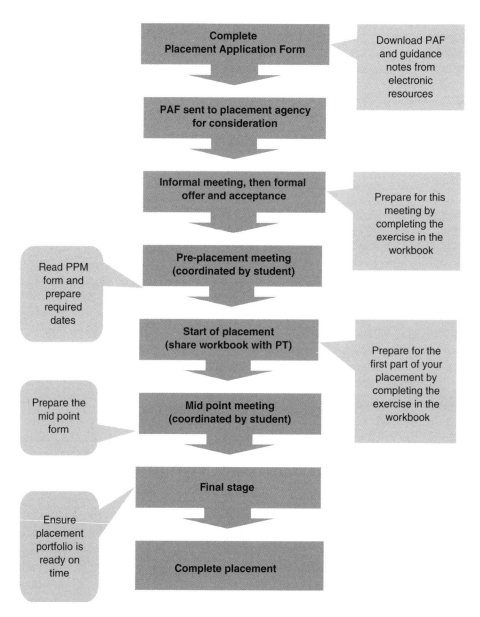

Figure 1.1   Example of the placement process at Manchester Metropolitan University (MMU) Social Work Programme. Reprinted with kind permission of Claire Bellamy at MMU and the Placement Team

carried out by the university placement team, and you will normally be required to complete the initial documentation online. The way in which you complete this should aim to open up your opportunities by stating your knowledge, skills, attributes, experience and learning needs, rather than specifying what type of placement you would prefer.

Once completed, the team will send out your request, usually to one placement agency that corresponds to the details you have stated on your form. Depending on the type of placement the request form may go through the local authority training section, e.g. social work; via education; to the training manager of a smaller non-statutory agency, e.g. Sure Start Project; to a single worker, e.g. Women's Aid or to a statutory enforcement agency, e.g. a prison or police force. Although it might seem that the agency is taking a long time to make a decision this is usually because they are negotiating the best type of service user group, team and practice educator to suit your learning needs and your experience. The placement personnel will be making a decision about whether they will offer you a placement solely on the basis of what you have written. Therefore, it is crucial that you make the best possible impression through the pro forma.

The simple diagram in Figure 1.1 shows the main organisational elements involved with placement management. Remember, you are central to this process so do get engaged with what is expected of you at each stage. Prepare questions beforehand and offer what you feel you can contribute. Express your enthusiasm to contribute to the team by sharing learning from the university, offering to create material to aid service users or conducting satisfaction surveys. Remember that some of the reasons that agencies offer placements are to keep them up-to-date with new thinking, theoretical applications and to have a neutral person who might be able to assess how well they are doing in the eyes of their service users. Whatever happens you can expect to take the lead at mid- and end-placement meetings, completing your placement documentation in advance of meetings, ensuring the relevant people have copies on the day and using your emotional intelligence to ensure the meetings and contacts with each stakeholder run smoothly. Here are some ideas to guide you.

ACTIVITY *1.5*

The first placement application form

Below is a placement request form completed by a Master's student for her first formal placement with an agency. With her permission I have adapted the information contained to anonymise the first placement agency and draw out elements of her thinking.

Imagine that you are a training officer for the agency to which this request has been forwarded for consideration. You decide what type of agency it is: statutory, voluntary, not-for-profit, charitable, non-statutory, third sector, private.

List the positive and negative attributes to the application and what information you think she should have included or excluded. How relevant would this application be in considering her for the placement?

Continued

ACTIVITY **1.5** *continued*

Manchester Metropolitan University

SOCIAL WORK PLACEMENT REQUEST FORM

Student profile

Areas of practice interest

I am passionate about becoming a social worker. Although I am interested in working with children and families as a possible future career path, I would like to use this 70-day placement opportunity to open up my knowledge about what social work entails. Not only as to the areas of practice available but also how my existing skills might be used and developed. Therefore, I am also interested in other areas, including mental ill health, youth justice, learning disabilities and domestic violence. Although these choices may seem rather disparate I have some experience of them all within my own family or friendships and my working and volunteering experiences.

Relevant experience (with dates from/to, to present)

Relief Support Worker (area given)

Generic Support Worker (area given)

Alcohol Intervention Worker (area given)

I currently work as a Support Worker, working with adults with learning disabilities and challenging behaviour. As part of my role, duties include support with personal care and household duties, support managing finances and taking medication and also support in the community whilst working in line with support programmes and risk assessments. As a Support Worker, I have worked independently and as part of a team; dependent on the service users' needs. The main priorities of my role are to promote independence and empower personal choice. In addition to this, integrating multi-agency working is also a key priority in order to provide a coherent and seamless service. As a Generic Support Worker, I worked particularly close with a service user who required constant one-to-one support. As a Relief Support Worker, I work across a number of different houses working with a range of service users with a range of needs.

As an Alcohol Intervention Worker, I worked frontline engaging with the community and those seen as 'hard to reach', offering a screening service to assess a person's alcohol consumption and drinking behaviour risk level, offering confidential advice, information, brief counselling and follow-up to ultimately improve health. The intervention service was offered on a one-to-one basis, group session or through facilitating workshops. Other responsibilities included organising my workload effectively in order to meet set targets and to continually build relationships

Continued

with other organisations to enable a quality service to be offered. Whilst working as an Alcohol Intervention Worker I also supported on other projects facilitating focus groups, phone interviews and analysing qualitative data.

Throughout all job roles, I have recorded information, written reports and communicated with colleagues through communication books, email, team meetings and face-to-face verbal communication.

Skills and knowledge

I feel I have a high level of communication and interpersonal skills, which enable me to communicate and relate well to others confidently. This is demonstrated through the range of people I have worked with in my previous and current employment, including service users with diverse needs and professional partners at a range of ages. I have worked with those socially excluded or facing social exclusion, those misusing substances and who have diverse health needs, and adults with learning disabilities. I have undertaken to attend training courses. These included motivational interviewing and cognitive behavioural therapy. This enabled me to apply theory to practice and to enable people to change their thinking processes, which affect their behaviour. I have taken part in focus group training which has helped to build on my skillset of facilitating group work. As a Support Worker, I work both as a lone worker and as part of a team, which demonstrates my ability to adapt to different work situations.

An important part of my role as an Alcohol Intervention Worker was to build and sustain relationships and partnerships with community organisations. I feel I demonstrated networking skills that resulted in a large web of networks being built and sustained since the project initially commenced as a pilot.

I have the ability to be non-judgemental and hold an empathetic view whilst also mainstreaming equality into all aspects of my work. I feel I am organised as I plan, monitor and review my work on a regular basis. I also have the ability to use my initiative demonstrated through my role as an Intervention Worker, as it was my responsibility to organise my own workload in order to meet objectives and targets.

Throughout my education, previous and current jobs, I have written detailed reports, recording and communicating vital aspects of my work. I also have extensive experience with computer programs.

Personal development is something I view as important; I am willing to take part in activities that build on this to develop my knowledge and skills.

Additional training and qualifications

I hold a Bachelor of Science Degree with Honours in Applied Psychology. I have also been trained in alcohol brief intervention, smoking cessation, focus group

Continued

ACTIVITY **1.5** *continued*

facilitation, motivational interviewing and cognitive behavioural therapy, as well as moving and handling.

Learning needs and areas for development on this placement

1. To deepen my experience and knowledge with service user groups either within new practice areas or at a more advance level in the areas of my existing expertise.

2. To develop skills around applying theory to practice and have the opportunity to evaluate effectiveness.

3. To develop assessment skills within agency, social policy and government guidance.

COMMENT

What sort of a picture do you have of this student? Has she presented her information in a way that shows she is using her existing skills and experience that equate with the social work task in your agency?

What if she had said that she wanted to qualify as a social worker so she could open a residential care facility for young people who had a learning disability – would that have been as convincing? Do you think that placement providers need to be able to assess a student's values – e.g. she said she was 'passionate' and she wanted to encourage 'independence'. She also mentioned that she is a good communicator and can work alone or in a team – what does that mean? Should she have placed more emphasis on being able to follow systems guidance, complete tasks on time and work on solutions rather than problems? Understanding what placement providers are looking for will help you to think through how to express your requirements and offers on the placement form.

Try asking yourself some critical questions.

For example:

1. What understanding do I have about the structures of the organisations that I would like to be placed with?

2. Do I need to do some research about this?

3. What advice do I need to seek from my tutor on how to express myself on the form?

4. How honest am I being about what sort of agencies I can expect to offer me a placement? Is my experience commensurate with their level of expectation of a student staff member?

5. How able am I to challenge any stereotypes I might have about certain placements and to turn these into opportunities?

You will see from the student's form that she has approached this with a balanced and realistic view of what she can offer, what she expects the placement to offer her and how she might set these opportunities within local, policy and governmental perspectives. She is flexible about the type of experiences she would like, either new or to deepen her current abilities, and shown that she realises the need for reflection, e.g. she asks to develop opportunities in evaluating her effectiveness. She has situated herself within her family, her knowledge and skills. She has been honest about her learning needs yet shown she has taken control of this with the use of technology. You might feel that she could have linked her experiences more closely with her skills, for example: 'In working closely with service users to enhance their empowerment I used advocacy skills in the promotion of self-advocacy. This involved me learning how to allow service users the space to express themselves whilst knowing when to prompt myself.'

It is now quite common for prospective practice placement agencies to ask students to visit for interview. Although this is often called an 'informal' visit, do be aware that you are being assessed and occasionally students are declined the placement on the grounds that it cannot offer the specific opportunities required by the student.

Reflecting on and rethinking placement offers

Think about the key dimensions of the placement offered to you.

1. Is this the right placement for you? If you have written broad and flexible statements about your requirements, existing skills, offers and hopes then the placement providers will be able to identify whether there is a role for you in their agency.

   Reflection – The placement agency is small and within the voluntary sector and I am not sure that I can gain experience as it is mainly run by volunteers. However, I found out that the volunteers are ex-users of the service and have received training. I think their personal experience will be invaluable to my learning and I can enhance their expertise by sharing relevant knowledge from the university.

2. Will you be able to evidence the key roles and the PCF? This means doing more than the minimum by using your creativity, professional artistry, integrating learning from university into the placement and taking opportunities to update colleagues on current research.

   Reflection – I do not think the placement has enough breadth and depth to enable learning experiences that will stretch me. However, I found out that the manager is a qualified psychotherapist and the deputy is an art therapist. I have a degree in music and would love to develop therapeutic methods through music to work with service users. I will think about how I could develop my music skills to complement the placement.

3. Will your learning needs and support requirements be met? Would it be possible to use sister agencies to gain additional experience and support? You will need to be proactive to ensure that your development needs will be met.

Reflection – I have worked for large insular authorities before and found that my creativity was suppressed in favour of form filling. At the informal meeting my practice teacher mentioned that much of their assessment work is contracted out to smaller community-based agencies where the hands-on work is done. I would love to take part in that and develop systems, courses and activities linked to the assessment of the service users.

These are all ways of positively rethinking placement offers using reflection. Remember that the placement team from the university will have confirmed that the placements they approach are able to offer learning opportunities and support commensurate with the professional requirements of the social work programme. To decline a placement because it does not appear to meet your learning needs in the first instance means that you will wait longer to be placed as the process will have to begin over again. It may also demonstrate that you feel some service users or agencies are not worthy of your involvement and/or that you are unable to think through initial impressions towards a creative approach to meeting your development needs.

ACTIVITY *1.6*

Creative dialogue to enhance placement experiences

In preparation for the pre-placement meeting with your tutor and practice educator (on-/off-site) re-read your placement application form (PAF).

1. *List the learning opportunities you would like to experience.*

2. *List the areas of your personal development that you would like to achieve.*

3. *Summarise and list the PCF and the HCPC codes of practice.*

COMMENT

During the meeting tick off those statements where there is a clear connection in the placement. Open up a dialogue to explore where the more obscure areas might be met and what plans would need to be put in place to ensure they happened. This might involve the practice teacher setting up strategies before you arrive or giving you contacts to pursue in your early weeks in placement. If you have done some preparation beforehand, for example, checked the agency publicity or website, you will be better informed to suggest alternatives and opportunities for your desired experiences.

Activities like the one above show you are fully engaged and enthusiastic about the placement and are professionally able to challenge statements where there does not appear to be any substance. For example, you want to work in child protection but are offered a placement in an adult drugs misuse agency. This involves completing risk assessments with the children of the service users. The on-site practice teacher reassures you that you would be able to undertake this work with the children in conjunction with a qualified staff member, where the work arises. That is great, but suppose none of the service users during your placement period have children – how would you gain experience of that work then? Might it be possible to link into a sister agency? Pursuing a line of enquiry in this way demonstrates that you are contemplating solutions from problems ahead, looking for alternative strategies, challenging in professionally acceptable ways and thinking through dilemmas. Of course, all things cannot be fully known at this stage and you will need to be mindful that you do not appear so demanding that the agency declines you on the grounds that it cannot meet your needs.

RESEARCH SUMMARY

Research was undertaken with 142 graduate social work students who had undertaken assessed practice placements to ascertain what contributed to their satisfaction. Although from America, and collated in 2008, the findings resonate with anecdotal feedback from students today in the UK.

Contributing most to satisfaction were students' perceptions of the quality of field instruction, the desirability of and involvement in the agency, and didactic explanations for (of) the field instructor. The findings highlight the importance of accessible supportive supervision, active learning, and feedback and conceptual input into student learning.

(Fortune and Abramson, 2008, pp95–110)

Additionally, Claudia Megele completed her Master's degree in social work at Goldsmiths, University of London in 2009.

Claudia reflected on the highly relevant area of 'praxis' in her placement and described this as the ability to relate theory and practice in a way that leads to informed action. She also shares a useful idea of involving practice agency staff with universities in order to share the tensions and dilemmas of contemporary practice.

Q: What were the most valuable things you learnt in your placements?

I realised that excellence in social work is a question of praxis (learning to apply the relevant theories and skills in your practice) rather than simple practice. I learnt that as a social worker you are constantly challenged to contain emotions and carry uncertainties, whilst maintaining a positive attitude and a solution-focused approach. The challenge is to translate theory into practical, effective and empowering solutions for your service users.

Q: Do you think the placement system was valuable?

Social work is a complex art and quite often involves balancing delicate issues. Therefore, it is essential that a student's knowledge of theory is grounded in practice, and quality placements are meant to do just that. Therefore, I think the placement system is not only valuable, but absolutely essential. It is only through real, on the job experience, that social workers can become true practitioners.

Continued

Q: Is there anything you would change about placements?

It would be good if there was greater coordination between universities and employers, particularly local authorities. For instance, universities could invite managers and frontline practitioners to share their experiences and dilemmas with students. This is important to ensure students keep in touch with the realities of practice and understand the intricacies of contemporary social work.

(The full review can be accessed at: www.socialworkconnections.org.uk/ features/158/a_social_work_student_reflects_on_her_placements)

CHAPTER SUMMARY

This chapter has begun to position your current learning by giving you guidance, information and areas for thought to support your approach towards your practice placements. In taking your learning forward you will begin to synthesise all that you are, your experience, knowledge, values and beliefs, aspirations and contributions and to frame your appreciation of enquiry, tensions and dilemmas ready for your social work placement. This has been the first step to taking your academic learning into practice and whichever placement it is you will be building on previous foundations. If you can visualise having a good archaeology (a firm base) from which to create your architecture (a strong building) you will go forward into your placement with confidence. It is to this area that we progress in Chapter 2.

FURTHER READING

Goleman, D (1998) *Working with Emotional Intelligence*. London: Bloomsbury.

A classic text to alert you to the enormous part that this subject plays in human communications. The essence is that any contact with other human beings involves us in making contact with the emotional currents that lie beneath our overt communications. This 'tap root' to deeper understanding has applications to all forms of contact, from the PAF through to highly complex child protection work. Along the way Goleman gives some enjoyable, humorous and illustrative examples to aid our understanding. Although developed for use in business, these skills are highly appropriate within social work.

Parker, J (2010) *Effective Practice Learning in Social Work*, 2nd edition. Exeter: Learning Matters.

Chapter 3 is dedicated to 'Preparing for practice' and integrates adult learning theories to help you to understand how to value your experiences and reflect on those you need to develop. Some guidance on how to create your personal learning plans is given and how to use these to negotiate the placement experience with your practice teacher.

USEFUL WEBSITES

www.communitycare.co.uk/articles/10/11/2010/115359/social-work-student-placement-guide.htm

This site has a guide to students going on placement and includes several links including 'tips from previous students' and 'how to get the best from your placements'.

www.theguardian.com/social-care-network/2012/oct/03/top-tips-social-work-students

A useful resource written by academics, practitioners and students including time management, flexibility and doing research.

Chapter 2

Understanding your placement through an organisational journey

This chapter will help you to develop the following capabilities, to the appropriate level, from the Professional Capabilities Framework:

- *Knowledge*: Demonstrate an initial understanding of the legal and policy frameworks and guidance that inform and mandate social work practice.
- *Contexts and organisations*: Demonstrate the impact of organisational context on social work practice.
- *Critical reflection and analysis*: Recognise and describe why evidence is important in social work practice.

It will also introduce you to the following standards as set out in the 2008 Social Work Subject Benchmark Statement:

4.7 Think critically about the complex social, legal, economic, political and cultural contexts in which social work practice is located.

5.1.1 The relationship between agency policies, legal requirements and professional boundaries in shaping the nature of services provided in interdisciplinary contexts and the issues associated with working across professional boundaries and within different disciplinary groups.

5.1.2 The contribution of different approaches to management, leadership and quality in public and independent human services.

5.1.4 Social science theories explaining group and organisational behaviour, adaptation and change.

5.1.5 The characteristics of practice in a range of community-based and organisational settings within statutory, voluntary and private sectors, and the factors influencing changes and developments in practice within these contexts.

5.2 Subject specific skills and the contexts in which they are applied.

Introduction

The focus of your thoughts leading up to beginning your placement is invariably about you and your needs. Once ensconced within your agency the locus shifts to the 'fit' between you, the agency, your colleagues and, not least, those who use the service. Your aim is to provide evidence that you are able to manoeuvre your way along the placement path, within the National Occupational Standards and code of ethics while dealing with the tensions and dilemmas created by the work and without straying too far from the boundaries of your organisation's cultural practices. Being on placement is rather like performing on one of those TV shows where you have to competently travel from A to B while remaining dry on top of a floating log, powered only by your legs and while balancing two dogs on each end of a log pole. Also, you must competently follow the rules of the game at the same time, e.g. within a set time, only going in a straight line and not falling off!

To support you in your placement journey this chapter will expose you to a variety of organisational management issues and dilemmas. These include strategies to challenge cultural practices that can exclude and discriminate against both students and service users. Competence across a variety of documentation will be examined and the appropriateness of language used for different purposes explored. The terminology of multi-professional working will be examined and the use of persuasive inclusivity will be applied to the benefit of those who use services. Skills of appreciative inquiry (AI) will infuse this chapter to include the development of strategies for organisational change. Critical discussion and practice examples will be seated in the legal mandates and policy guidance that underpin professional practice across the sector.

By the end of this chapter you will be able to:

- critically analyse a variety of organisational cultures and practices;
- assess and critique a variety of documentation formats used by agencies;
- appreciate and seek information through a range of multi-professional and collaborative activities;
- be aware of some of the legislation/policy that informs and gives legal power to your practice.

Organisational games (cultural practices)

Previously I mentioned the need to follow the rules of the game. Try to think about your placement organisation as having a set of rules. These may be formal, informal or anecdotal. They will have been established in law, policy guidance, custom and practice and agency structure, using theories of organisational change and through a consideration of the social psychology of human management. Of particular relevance is the area of knowledge around human relations, and the structural analysis of social networks.

RESEARCH SUMMARY

Organisational culture and job satisfaction

Flap and Volker (2001) examined what influenced job satisfaction through assessing the existence of job specific social capital. They found that the ties between a person's social capital at work and their network produced well-being and social approval. For example, when the goal was to search for resources within their networks people used networks that promoted:

Continued

- *satisfaction with aspects of the job such as income, career opportunities and security. For example, a large local authority employer would offer career progression with opportunities for enhancement with pensions and security of tenure.*

- *belonging to closed networks of identity-based solidarity such as the social climate at work, cooperation with management and colleagues. For example, professionally specific groups would give affirmative support and solidarity.*

- *crucial ties between a focal actor linking two or more exclusive cliques (negative effect) or between familiar and trusting groups (positive effect). Links between health, social care, education and housing may be tied by time-limited project work, for example in substance misuse, where the director controls the resources and personnel from differing professional fields and where there are varying levels of trust and expertise.*

Masterson et al. (2000) linked the notion of individual social capital – the sense of self-worth and inherent power to achieve change, with the existence of a sense of 'procedural and interactional justice' between supervisor and member within the work environment. The authors termed this 'interactional justice' and found that staff who felt the organisation and their supervisor supported them were more likely to be positive about working to achieve organisation-led outcomes.

A previous piece of work by Podolny and Baron (1997) had examined the place of social networks within the workplace. They found that a large yet sparse network of informal ties was required to get information and resources, whereas a small and dense network was better to promote better knowledge of one's role performance requirements. So there is certainty in having clear role boundaries and expectations from close colleagues while simultaneously having access to information and resources through wider informal links. Your task is to develop these types of social networks in the placement organisation.

Placement organisational cultures

The development of your own social capital in the workplace will be influenced by the organisational culture of your placement and, by definition, the types of employees it has created. It is worth saying that self-reflection and critical self-analysis are axiomatic to your development in the placement. Understanding, moulding, adapting, learning and challenging behaviours should be subject to your personal regime of self-analysis. This understanding of self can then be used as a lens through which to view your organisational culture.

The organisational cultures of statutory agencies and the larger charities undertaking social work have generally conformed to hierarchical structures in the belief that the span of control is more effective through the 'unity of command' established by Henri Fayol (Pugh and Hickson, 2007, quoted in Adams et al., 2009a, chapter 9). Fayol stated that each worker should be responsible to one supervisor from whom orders were delegated. Weber had previously identified hierarchies as perfect organisations, being managed by workers with commensurate expertise, specialisation and role boundaries. However, they were also characterised by being impersonal, alienating, developing a life of their own, inflating rules larger than their original purpose and allowing those in managerial positions to perpetuate their own importance by controlling access to information crucial to the running of the organisation. These latter qualities suppressed any democratisation and led to self-perpetuating managerial control. It can be seen that 'managerialism' has firmly established such a place in social work agencies.

So it is that social workers working in the statutory field are enmeshed within a plethora of rules, systems, custom and practice, law, policy and procedures that are frequently managed through the completion of documentation. Directives are issued top-down with little opportunity for bottom-up feedback. Alternatively, social work has seen the movement of task-centred human services out of bureaucracies into the organic structures of the voluntary and smaller charitable sector. Their accountability trail, although dealing with some aspects of form-filling linked to funding, has taken on a more organic structure placing process and user involvement at the centre of a more human relations school of management. Dennis Saleebey (1995) has written of the strengths perspective in social work where 'developmental resilience, healing and wellness, and constructionist narrative and story have provided interesting supports and challenges'. Differing from the pyramidal structures of hierarchies, such organisations work with a flat structure where decisions are owned by management, staff and service users and ideas and evaluations can flow freely through the organisation.

Within the multi-professional approaches of more 'joined-up' service provision specialisations are becoming blurred and access to multi-disciplinary education, training and development is demystifying, or weakening depending on your point of view, the once ring-fenced bodies of professional knowledge that acted to protect professionals or exclude service users. New terms such as 'what works', 'communities of practice', best value', 'user choice', 'purchaser and provider', 'job satisfaction', 'value added' are used to signify new ways of working, moving away from the manufacturing roots of organisational management theory.

As we have moved into the twenty-first century, information technology has revolutionised how we work across all occupations and you will notice this not least when you visit your placement for the first time. Social work appears to have become a computer-based activity, with offices full of banks of computers where highly qualified social workers sit extracting and inputting data.

Looking to the future, Moynagh and Worsley (2005, pp118–19, in Adams et al., 2009a, pp109–10) foresee five styles of organisations that would be best suited to social work:

1. the virtual corporation, 'a network of contractors held together by legal bonds' or joint venture agreements, coordinated through a 'strategic centre'. For example, research organisations on poverty or health inequalities;

2. the boundaryless organisation or one with 'highly porous' boundaries and greater use of internal and external networks, in which 'information will flow freely across its "borders" and people will work easily on either side.' For example, organisations working with the effects of the globalisation of trafficking;

3. the project-based (or team) organisation, made up of temporary groups of people that will disperse as the project ends. For example, certain virtual communities of practice that might form to merge the functions of health and social care;

4. the modular (or cellular) corporation, in which small teams with standard operating procedures combine and recombine in different configurations. For example, in the reorganisation of health and social care service provision, self-sufficient groups might come together to work on services for dementia sufferers;

5. the process-based (or horizontal) organisation, which will manage processes not functions. For example, the process for staff development linked to the Professional Capabilities Framework and which you will experience as an NQSW in your ASYE.

Critical questions about placement cultures

What critical questions should contemporary social workers raise about the nature of their work within agencies? Here are some suggestions.

1. How can professional artistry, e.g. creativity and the notion of 'masterly' work, replace technical rationalism, e.g. functionalism and conformity, where a paper trail of accountability must be evidenced? If Newly Qualified Social Workers are to use their emotional intelligence to ensure a sensitivity to service user involvement, how is it possible to log this in a system that tends to focus on efficiency of outcome rather than process?

2. Are the processes of collaborative working across disciplinary boundaries conducive to information sharing?

3. What cooperative structures could be created that would be helpful in forming partnerships?

4. What benefits/drawbacks can be offered by the security of process (e.g. larger charities and statutory work) or innovations that are more tenuous yet can respond quickly to new social problems?

5. What concerns do the services of social entrepreneurs pose for my value base, because profit is their focus?

6. What effect does working in a 'risk society' have on the nature of accountability and the creation of yet more documentation to absolve practitioners of blame?

These are just a few of the considerations that you might think about when developing your reflective approach to practice. These types of questions lift you above the functional approaches of merely focusing on the outcomes by pushing your thinking from the micro (person/family) to the macro (network/system) agendas and back again. In between you will also become aware of the meso (inter-connectedness) level.

Now, apply these critical questions to how John in Case Study 2.1 could think about his practice within a statutory organisation. You do not need to be concerned with finding the answers but more with the debates the questions raise and subsequent further questions they create for you.

CASE STUDY 2.1

Critical questions and organisational considerations in practice

John began his placement in a local authority older persons' team linked to hospital discharge. All was well until his practice educator raised some concerns at the mid-placement meeting. She said John was having difficulty grasping the nature of the work and needed to gain focus within this fast-paced team if he was not to fail. He was spending time contacting service users after discharge. John was devastated by this news and afterwards raised this with his tutor as he felt undermined and his confidence was shaken.

COMMENT

John's previous experience had been in the voluntary sector where he had his first placement but also had based this on his volunteering work with young adults who had a learning disability. He had been applauded for his interest in following up referrals rigorously to ensure that service users had received appropriate services promptly and he had visited after a few weeks to ensure the services were satisfactory and to make further requests for services where needed. He had developed personal networks with other service provider colleagues and had been highly accountable for his practice to his immediate supervisor in the voluntary sector agency. It appeared that the skills needed for his current placement were entirely different. He was expected to complete a discharge assessment document and expedite this quickly. It was not considered his role to check that the community social worker had carried out his referral nor to check with the service user that all was satisfactory on, and following, discharge. There was a high element of the 'revolving door' syndrome causing frequent hospital readmissions but the hospital social work team felt powerless to make representation about this to the medical team who were seen to be above them in the medical hierarchy.

John was only allowed to share minimal information within a limited box on the electronic discharge form. He was required to use a certain form of words to describe the services needed that also used a formulaic approach to the identification, assessment and management of risk.

The service had been commissioned by the health authority to make assessments of risk and mental capacity and there was no remit to create time for development of the skills or systems of collaborative working. Staff saw their social work role as doing the bidding of the hospital discharge service and felt powerless to suggest the development of a more collaborative partnership role. While they felt that they were well supported by the bureaucratic documentation in relation to risk and blame they were unable to

Continued

COMMENT continued

respond innovatively to new social problems in their field and so maintained their current documentation that was quickly out of date.

The student had worked on brokerage in his previous placement, linking into some exciting private provision run by social entrepreneurs from which he commissioned innovative services for younger disabled people. His current placement was tied into very conventional services that were subject to local contracting arrangements and that lacked any possibility for innovation.

REFLECTION POINT

Here are some of John's reflective questions on his organisation's practice. Do you agree with his choice of questions? Can you think of any more?

1. *Why do I feel such dissonance with the organisation in this placement?*

2. *How might I raise this with my practice teacher without being critical of my on-site supervisor?*

3. *What strategies for change might I suggest as a student in this placement?*

4. *What learning might I take from this situation into my first employment as an NQSW?*

COMMENT

John was a highly committed student who was always anxious to do his very best in every aspect of university and practice life. He was very considerate of all other aspects of his life, always striving to do the best in all his relationships. The criticism from his practice teacher had shaken him to the core and caused him to question his ability to judge his performance. One could say that he needed to have some of these sensibilities shaken out of him to make him stronger and in order to bear the emotional content of his work. If this was the case the practice educator should have raised these issues in supervision and not exposed him in this way at the mid-placement meeting. This is a point John might want to take up in his next supervision session with her.

Research links: social capital

In terms of Flap and Volker's study, John gained social capital through completing his MA and, therefore, establishing his career prospects. However, there was a mismatch in his relationship with his practice educator who felt his relationships should remain loyal to the team and not develop the larger network with service users and other providers.

In doing this he would need to try to de-personalise how he feels by using language such as: 'Can we take some time to discuss how I should deal with my feelings about wanting to follow up discharges to ensure service users are okay as I do understand the fast-paced nature of the placement?' In this way John is owning his feelings rather than criticising the practice educator or the placement practices. Later, when he feels more confident, he might try to ascertain whether this is policy or just the team's reaction to pressure.

Research links: the impact of belonging

John might reflect on the Flap and Volker findings in assessing the impact of belonging to (a) a close-knit identity-based group around management and colleagues as opposed to (b) between two or more exclusive cliques where the researchers found a negative impact. Although these two roles of the focal contact person are necessary they lack congruence in that (a) is secure whereas (b) is tenuous. John felt in control of his role within the social work team but unsure of his role in relation to interacting with doctors, health visitors and external support teams. However, when challenged by his practice educator this stability was undermined.

John might share his practice of following up referrals while in his voluntary sector role and ask if this might be something that students might be allowed to do in the hospital placement to gain experience. He could make the case for this by suggesting that where the referred-to service knows they will be contacted, they will ensure adequate provision is put in place. Also where service users are followed up by the hospital discharge service, they will have continuity through discharge.

Research links: interactional justice

John could learn from Masterson's research (Masterson et al., 2000) about the nature of interactional justice in the development of his social capital in the workplace. He could argue the case for a student role that enveloped external relations that could potentially change the established ways of working. An example would be to see if more diligent follow-up of discharged persons might reduce the recurrence of admission. This would enhance the medical opinion of the effect social work had on their service to the extent that readmissions were reduced leading to budget savings.

The learning John takes from this to his first employment as an NQSW would be to develop his social networks whether spread out and sparse or close-knit and intense, to learn about types of practice. This could encompass what is used and what might be developed to enhance service provision and organisational efficacy, the latter being subject to techniques of AI in organisational change and personal well-being.

Research links: networks in working cultures

Podolny and Baron (1997) give clear guidelines as to the use of both close and extended networks in working cultures and, through his awareness of such, John would be able to develop and apply these throughout his working life.

An understanding of the mesh of organisational complexities is vital if you are to find your place within the placement agency. Be prepared to seek guidance on these issues rather than expose yourself to criticism that you might feel is unjust. One way to open up debate about organisational processes is to cast a critical eye over the paperwork used.

And now the paper work

Here is a quote from Jan Little, a freelance trainer:

> *It's performance management, these days. It's crisis work. It's case management – we don't actually work with people any more. It's all paperwork. It's telling people what they can't have.*

(www.hgi.org.uk/archive/social-work2.htm#.Uv1Z_3nVuf0)

The nature of social work across all fields began to change with the need to demonstrate effective, efficient and accountable provision. The demise of trust and the emergence of litigation within social work, coupled with new funding mechanisms, means that many practitioners feel that increasingly eligibility criteria are fashioned to exclude access to provision. Hence the above quote – 'it's telling people what they can't have'.

However, the practicalities of performance management through targets and performance indicators, timescales and framework mapping tools form an important part of the management structures and, through these, provide accountability streams to government. This can be considered as only one half of the equation, with the professional artistry of the social worker balancing out the second half. This second stream would encapsulate the values and ethics of social work in challenging oppression and discrimination, ensuring the service user is central to any assessment. The nature of the social work task then becomes a part of the human givens about how equilibrium can be created not only for service user needs but also for the needs of the social worker. This is a recognition of your social, emotional and psychological needs as a professional and throughout your career.

Figure 2.1 indicates that an integration of both left and right hemispheres of our brain is needed to function with equilibrium in professional life and within the organisations in which we work. This is not only applicable to social work and with the increasing demand for accountability through documentation, we can use our creative side to challenge the sterility of the information it produces. These skills remain with us through progression through the PCF and, with luck, will be influential at higher levels indicated by progression to strategic leadership in education, principal practitioner or manager.

Assessing the documentation

This is another quote from Jan Little:

> *I am not saying that social work is over-controlled. Indeed, I strongly believe that social work needs to be evidence-based and accountable, which inevitably means a certain amount of record keeping. However, tick box forms completed*

Functional abilities ⟵⟶ Creative abilities

Factual, logical, detail oriented, knows the truth, values order, strategic, safe, practical, objective

Imaginative, intuitive, acknowledges feelings, sees alternatives, philosophical, appreciates debate, allows risks to be taken, subjective

Social work student on placement

Newly Qualified Social Worker

Assessed and Supported Year in Employment

Social Worker

Experienced Social Worker

Social Work Educator, Advanced Social Work Practitioner, Social Work Manager

Strategic Social Work Educator, Principal Social Worker, Strategic Social Work Manager

Development of Advanced Thinking

Layers of progression

Continuing Professional Development (CPD)

Application of the Professional Capabilities Framework

Figure 2.1   The social worker within their professional domain

> *in duplicate may show we visited a particular family at a particular time and we actually saw the child in question, but they are absolutely no help in determining whether what we did on the visit was in any way effective.*

(www.hgi.org.uk/archive/social-work2.htm#.Uv1Z_3nVuf0)

I am sure this quote may have some resonance for those of you in placement. You know that you must complete the correct documentation appropriately yet feel there would be a better way to use a more narrative approach to an assessment. You might also wonder how the form came about, as it seems so functional and does not give any opportunity for the expression of aims, goals and stages, to indicate successful outcomes for the service user.

In completing initial/risk/eligibility assessments it is vital to remember that any reviewing worker or panel will rely on your summing up of the service user's situation. If you feel that 'the form didn't ask that question', or 'there was nowhere to put what the person said', then you are not truly representing their view and this will disadvantage them in receiving services. Similarly, you might feel that the documentation poses questions in a certain way that could lead to misrepresentation of the service user's needs. For example, 'When did you stop beating your wife?' invites some reference to the fact that the wife was beaten rather than when it ceased.

Taking the two extreme examples shown in Figures 2.2 and 2.3, we can look at social work documentation both as a legal document and one that includes service user and carer views.

Check List:

☐ Medication list (what & why)

☐ Home medical equipment

☐ Community resources

☐ Getting home (how & who)

☐ Visiting nurse service in place?

☐ Special diet

☐ Follow-up appointments

☐ Rehab requirements

☐ Mobility limitations (stairs, driving)

☐ Wound care

Figure 2.2   Example A: a hospital discharge assessment list for a frail older man

Source: www.incareofdad.com/blog/hospital-discharge-planning-may-be-dangerous-to-your-health

---

CAF assessment summary: strengths and needs

Consider each of the elements to the extent they are appropriate in the circumstances. You do not need to comment on every element. Wherever possible, base comments on evidence, not just opinion, and indicate what your evidence is. However, if there are any major differences of view, these should be recorded too.

1. **Development of unborn baby, infant, child or young person**

Health

General health

Conditions and impairments; access to and use of dentist, GP, optician; immunisations, developmental checks, hospital admissions, accidents, health advice and information

---

(Continued)

Figure 2.3 (Continued)

Physical development

Nourishment; activity; relaxation; vision and hearing; fine motor skills (drawing etc.); gross motor skills (mobility, playing games and sport, etc.)

Speech, language and communication

Preferred communication, language, conversation, expression, questioning; games; stories and songs; listening; responding; understanding

Emotional and social development

Feeling special; early attachments; risking/ actual self-harm; phobias; psychological difficulties; coping with stress; motivation, positive attitudes; confidence; relationships with peers; feeling isolated and solitary; fears; often unhappy

Behavioural development

Lifestyle, self-control, reckless or impulsive activity; behaviour with peers; substance misuse; anti-social behaviour; sexual behaviour; offending; violence and aggression; restless and overactive; easily distracted, attention span/concentration

Figure 2.3 Example B: the Common Assessment Framework taken from Every Child Matters (an 11-page initial assessment of which this is one page)

Source: http://webarchive.nationalarchives.gov.uk

As you will realise, these two types of assessment format seem to be at the extremes of accountability and control. Example A is highly practical yet neglects to address any user/carer concerns, while example B gives detailed information elicited from the service user or carer. A further section on the form requires the completion of boxes regarding outcomes, action, who and when, and portrays a highly controlling approach to be taken by the professional social worker completing the form.

ACTIVITY 2.1

Critiquing the organisational pro formas A and B

Here is another quote from Jan Little:

> Unfortunately, with tick box tools, there is always the risk of their being misused and completed mechanically. Some social workers feel that completing the assessment records consumes too much time because so much information is required.

> *(www.hgi.org.uk/archive/social-work2.htm#.Uv1Z_3nVuf0)*

This implies that the routine of a tick box instrument leads to complacency and simplistic responses whereas more in-depth and lengthy examples take up too much time out of a busy schedule. Often being completed online they also demonstrate that social workers spend the majority of their time in front of computers rather than the face-to-face preferred method of 'working with people'. In analysing the two examples of assessment documentation A and B:

(a) Think critically about what advantages there are to each process.

(b) What elements should go into an assessment pro forma that encompass both the flexibility of a more naturalistic approach using a service user narrative and the need for accountability and conformity with legal responsibilities?

COMMENT

Would it be helpful if the assessee (service user or carer, or advocate in the case of a young child or person without mental capacity) were given the opportunity to complete parts of the documentation themselves with support?

This might give more weight to their views but what might be the legal implications for the worker and agency? Mainly the legislation refers to the service user's right to an assessment or in the case of vulnerability, to protection. The social worker responses resulting from completing the list (example A) or documentation (example B) might go some way towards demonstrating whether there is evidence that the correct procedures under law have been shown. Yet, what is the purpose of this for the service user? Is it a procedure that only serves a functionalist perspective for the agency or worker?

Some writers on this subject would say that the bureaucratic nature of agency documentation serves to protect service user rights and protect the vulnerable. The NIHCE (2011) guidance for adult mental health services does include that service users must be given a copy of their care plan, but notes that it is not their property even though it is all about them. It also states that one way to evaluate the position regarding control and restraint would be to encourage service users to write notes on their experience to be shared with professionals within multi-agency and multi-disciplinary approaches. Retrospectively, this does nothing to improve their experience but uses their knowledge and intellectual property to improve training for those who might be part of the problem. This experience of

Continued

discrimination (treating someone badly because of who they are) exacerbates the generally oppressive experience – how services are constructed, for those who use mental health services.

*In some documentation the assessment language or acronyms used exclude non-professionals; even advocates need to ask for clarification. The People First service user movement developed clever visual ways for assessment documentation, using mainly visual symbols based on their inclusivity for those who found their position difficult to vocalise or to write about. The People First Group in Bury did this to discuss their views on service provision. You can view this at: **www.bury.gov.uk/CHttpHandler.ashx?id=7607&p=0**.*

The fact is that official documents serve to protect both workers and service users when they provide evidence of time and place, information gathered according to the law, assessment of risk, capability, aspirations and future action to support or compel. Essentially the documents should support the assessment rather than the assessment supporting the documentation, and include a clear service user perspective even where there is disagreement. If your interview technique is solely around gathering information for the documentation then you need to consider whose purpose this is serving and whether the act itself is oppressive.

Challenging agency documentation through the application of appreciative inquiry (AI) and emotional intelligence (EI)

The skill of achieving change using AI is to know how to ask powerful questions. These lead us to say 'What if?/So what now?' rather than 'Yes/No or Who/When'. There are similarities with the Critical Questions Framework used in my first text, *Critical Learning for Social Work Students*, in which I posed the idea of four types of questions that would build a scaffold for learning to be more critical (Table 2.1).

Table 2.1   Stages towards asking critical questions

Question type	Description	Attribute
Fundamental	What do I think/know about X?	Describing, underpinning points with quotations.
Connecting	How does X relate to Y and Z?	Judging, balancing different perspectives, identifying a major contender in the debate.
Hypothesis	If X relates to Y and Z, then A	Consolidation, creativity, positioning a new perspective.
Critical	How can I defend my argument in evaluating X, Y, Z and A?	Contemplation, lateral thinking, conceptualisation of micro and macro debates and posing insightful explanations, solutions and/or challenges.

Questions that use AI are thought provoking and broaden, deepen and focus the debate. They invite reflection and a move to reflexive practice and critical understanding. They stimulate curiosity and creativity and can expose underlying assumptions. They would expose and deconstruct the discourses that underpin the areas of questioning. More about the development of questions using AI to develop powerful questions can be found at: **http://design.umn.edu/about/ intranet/documents/AppreciativeInquiry-Asking%20Powerful%20Questions.pdf**.

The process of using AI as an organisational change strategy would be to decide on what the end result might be by working with a small number of colleagues to create a number of relevant questions.

REFLECTION POINT

Go back to the CAF form on page 36 and look at the descriptors on which the assessor should question the service user or their advocate under the 'emotional and social development' heading.

1. *What underlying assumptions does asking questions on these areas imply?*

2. *Where has it come from?*

3. *Whose purpose does it serve?*

4. *How might the child/young person be better represented in it?*

5. *How might questioning be better expressed to encapsulate the strengths and aspirations of the child?*

Seven of the descriptors are negative (risk, phobia, psychological difficulties, stress, feelings of isolation and being solitary, having fears and often unhappy). Three are positive (feeling special, motivation and positive) and three are neutral (early attachments, relationships with peers and confidence). Does this lead to a tendency to focus on the negative side of the child's experiences and character? A child may feel special through being groomed, so the interpretation is not so straightforward. Feelings of isolation or being solitary need not be a negative experience – we are not all group animals. If a child is very interested in dissecting insects does this signify cruelty or an enquiring mind? Subjective judgements led by such questions are often made by the social worker/carer. Might it be better to give the child the opportunity to present some of their narrative, drawings, diary or notes as part of the assessment to be considered holistically by the assessment team?

If your aim was to begin by thinking creatively about what end you would prefer to have in this documentation, setting the child/advocate at the core of a positive assessment process with evidence, views and judgements from interested others on the periphery, then this would ensure a more child-centred approach to the assessment. Working with interested others to construct several questions would enable scope, reflection and creativity to be included centrally. For example, cultural constructions could be explored that may avoid the recent 'sensitivity' that was exposed in the failure to take action in the grooming of white teenage girls and boys in Rochdale and Cambridge. One of the great revelations to most teachers in higher education is that it is not so important to know the answers as to ask the incisive question. These are questions that make us think, expose our biases and myths and cause us to question our own truths. They lead to new, and often revelational shifts in consciousness that thrust our learning forward. By using these techniques of AI to challenge agency documentation we can ensure that service user views, wants and needs are axiomatic to their own assessments and do not perpetuate the bureaucratic functionalism that often second guesses their needs by leading questions.

ACTIVITY **2.2**

Using appreciative inquiry (AI) to change discriminatory practice

Focusing on the following three different types of assessment used in adult care work create one AI question for each.

1. *To assess eligibility. The form asks: 'Are you able to wash yourself?'*

2. *To assess risk. The form asks: 'How many falls have you had in the past month?'*

3. *To potentially limit autonomy. The form asks: 'Do you have suicidal thoughts?'*

COMMENT

Turning around the wording of these questions would focus the power more on the service user's own description of their needs rather than agency questions pre-empting a response. For example:

1. *Tell us about any difficulties you have in managing your personal care, for example bathing, washing yourself or dressing.*

The purpose of this question is to find out whether the person meets the eligibility criteria for services, and is not necessarily so narrow as to enquire only about washing.

Question 2 is really asking whether the person is in any risk: perhaps they live alone and may injure themselves or die if services are not provided. Yet is this question also about risk to the agency of not providing services? Older people are often reluctant to declare risky situations for fear of being coerced into residential care. Risk has been proven to be lessened if there is a supportive network around the person, e.g. milk person or neighbour alerted to phone a contact number when milk is not collected or curtains remain undrawn during the day. So risk can be ameliorated and balanced with a person's right to choose to live in a situation where daily risk will occur. So question 2 may read:

2. *What sort of things have happened to you in your home where it would have been helpful to have some urgent help? Possibly when you have been unsteady or dizzy?*

In asking question 3 the purpose may be to limit the individual's action to take their own life, and to demonstrate that this should be done through a compulsory admission to hospital. Research has shown that having autonomy strengthens older people, their dignity and respect in later life and that these are traits that may lessen the risk of suicide

Continued

(Vanlaere et al., 2007). Might it be better to ask such questions and consequent upon the answers to build support networks around such people to enhance these qualities? In this case the question might read:

3. *Tell us how we might help you to cope better, for example, to help you to do things for yourself more, to feel proud and confident, and to know that others think well of you.*

Developing an emotional intelligence (EI) repertoire in professional competence

The other quality closely allied to criticality in practice within organisations is EI. Daniel Goleman (1998) devised five skill sets for personal and social competence from which he identified 25 subthemes and 93 competence descriptors (Table 2.2).

Table 2.2   Daniel Goleman's five skill sets for EI

Personal competence	Social competence
Self-awareness – emotional awareness, accurate self-assessment, self-confidence	Social awareness – empathy, service orientation, developing others, leveraging diversity, political awareness
Self-regulation, self-control, trustworthiness, conscientiousness, adaptability, innovation	Social skills – influence, communication, leadership, change catalyst, conflict management, building bonds, collaboration and cooperation, team capabilities
Self-motivation – achievement, drive, commitment, initiative, optimism	

(For further explanation of AI and EI, see Jones (2013, pp93–104).)

These abilities, although originally applied to the world of business in America, are clearly central to any work within human enterprises and professions. If one wishes to change/confirm organisational practices then the competences of EI must be applied to AI. The management of the organisation and of the social work taking place within it is both complementary and contested. Social workers are employees to be managed within the organisation but at the same time must manage themselves, their caseloads and the supply of services to their users. Herein exists a tension where those on the frontline, the social workers, see better ways to create and deliver services that reflect need, whereas their managers' focus lies in accountability, transparency, efficiency and effectiveness. Frequently these two agendas appear to be in conflict, yet the rationality of management and the liberation of anti-oppressive practice of social workers must meet at the point of balance. This means that service users will feel confident that employees are under control and being professionally supervised while at the same time working to facilitate their human rights and dignity. Social workers who apply their EI to these situations will be able to deal with the dilemmas posed by their work and reduce stress levels. Understanding why the agencies operate as they do will release the worker from the anxiety of conflict onto a conflict resolution trajectory in which EI and AI form the theoretical basis for change. A dissonance of practice is often highlighted by the need to share information and work across professional boundaries. It is to this area we now move.

Organisational issues in multi-agency practice

Also referred to as multi-professional and multi-disciplinary working, multi-agency practice follows recent government policy of information sharing to ensure that service users do not fall between service gaps or are susceptible to risk and danger. This strategy has raised ethical questions for social workers, community workers, educational establishments and the medical profession, support services, residential care, the police and probation services. In fact, it remains a bone of contention for most organisations because of service user confidentiality.

ACTIVITY 2.3

Ruth's rehabilitation

At the age of 16 Ruth had become pregnant and been placed in residential care being considered to be at risk of sexual exploitation. She was told her baby was delivered still-born. She later became pregnant again while living in care and again was told that her baby did not survive. You have been allocated her case to rehabilitate Ruth into sheltered accommodation at the age of 64 because the care home is closing following the Care in the Community initiative. In the file you read that both Ruth's children survived and were sent for adoption.

What are the implications for Ruth, you as the worker, your agency and Ruth's children and possibly grandchildren?

COMMENT

What information would you consider it was appropriate to share and with whom? To whom is it appropriate – the service user, the agency, you as a worker, your manager or supervisor? What would be your purpose in sharing and through what method would you do so – a report, a common management information system (e.g. computer storage system), verbally, by email? What information might you decline to share and how would you argue your case to do so? Should the children (now adults and perhaps parents themselves) be traced and would Ruth have a right to know about any grandchildren she might have?

Your agency might consider that the purpose of your intervention was to establish Ruth in community accommodation and provide any support necessary for that. The issue of potentially having a family might be considered out of your remit. Yet service users have rights to access information held about them. Would you consider encouraging Ruth to read her file? What might be the consequences for all concerned?

Multi-disciplinary skills within organisational policy

As I previously mentioned, organisational structures in social work are changing. Teams may be created and disbanded to deal with single issues. There may be a joining of disciplines, say social work and education, social work and health, where workers have been trained in differing values and subject matter. In safeguarding work there will be a requirement to work with other relevant professional fields to ensure holistic assessments where service users do not fall between services. There might even be a perceived hierarchy of power where professionals view themselves as having more kudos, for example consultants over social work or statutory over voluntary sector provision. Whatever your placement agency you are likely to find that multi-disciplinary working is central to your skills repertoire. The areas of such practice will depend on the purpose, professional focus, policies and structure of the agency.

The organisational language used to refer to those it serves will depend on what type of organisation or agency it is. How those receiving services are called is socially constructed within a network of professional power and societal expectations. So it is that 'patients' receive help in hospitals and clinics and are supported by medical staff. 'Clients' may go to advocates, solicitors and counsellors and 'service users' to social workers. Other terms such as 'customer', 'member', and 'friend' are often used within the voluntary sector where they are seen to be more inclusive and less stigmatising. These terms are underpinned by the values that workers hold and the beliefs about how those they work with should be helped. It is vital that you familiarise yourself with these agendas and with the professional remit and boundaries of the other disciplines and services you work with.

As social workers we need to use our EI to key into these different professional discourses and appreciate the variety of approaches that can be mobilised in support of our service users. This means developing an inclusive rather than blaming method of working across professional boundaries, yet knowing when to deal with unprofessional practice. A social worker's stance can be described as supportive yet sceptical – weighing the need for nurture and care with rationality and evidence.

Here are some ideas from my own practice:

Kinga, a young person with learning disability, is refused access to a college course.

Strategies:

- Contact the college special needs advisor and ask to review the college mission statement with them.

- Invite the advisor to work collaboratively with you to ascertain why the decision to refuse Kinga access to the course was made.

- Analyse how the decision(s) might be (a) challenged or (b) defended. In the case of (b) set about deconstructing each claim to create opportunities for Kinga to gain any compensatory skills or experience.

- Involve the Gateway centre staff who are able to offer additional support in achieving this and in giving their opinions as to Kinga's abilities.

- Recruit an advocate from Citizen Advocacy and support Kinga in joining her local People First group.

- Construct a network map showing Kinga within her local support network, indicating where she would like more or less input/contact to enable her to attend college. Review this each month for three months to show how changes are occurring.

ACTIVITY 2.4

Skills in multi-disciplinary practice

What are the skills in multi-disciplinary practice that the social worker used in the above plan?

COMMENT

Collaboration and cooperation are essential to open up a dialogue with the college to expose the real reasons, e.g. lack of pre-requirements or discrimination, for refusing Kinga a place.

The language used should be carefully chosen to **create an inclusive dialogue**:

> 'I am sure it was not intentional to exclude Kinga due to her disability so can we look at strategies to break down the skills she would need for this course and then go about ensuring she has the opportunity to acquire them.'

Of course, this is not to say that every opportunity is open to everyone. I might want to be an astronaut or a brain surgeon but have neither the ability nor the stamina, even with training! So part of multi-disciplinary working is to **be realistic about what can be achieved through fair access and anti-discriminatory practice**.

Creating a supportive network is central to multi-disciplinary practice. It is not necessary to have a multitude of professionals intervening but to have an advisory team backing up a frontline worker. In Kinga's case it may be more appropriate for her advocate to follow through with support but have other professionals and voluntary personnel available to advise.

The social worker and the college special needs advisor must be able to **cross their professional boundaries**. The special needs coordinator would have to research and ascertain why the decisions had been made to exclude Kinga and to challenge these where appropriate. The social worker began to delve into planning for new educational experiences that could raise Kinga's skills to the pre-requisite level.

This strategy may have opened up the **flexibility of new opportunities** for Kinga within the college basic skills courses. These connections between the special needs coordinator and the social worker would focus on **potential benefits in the long**

Continued

term for other service users. Their relationship developed a **point of contact for both**, the college tutor to refer students who might be in need of support and a direct link to young people with special needs looking to attend college. This becomes a truly collaborative relationship **creating added value** to both agencies.

These interpersonal relationships go **underneath the management structures** and create a network of multi-agency, multi-professional and multi-disciplinary cooperation that is difficult to legislate for.

Robert Adams (Adams et al., 2009a, p28) refers to people who have **good boundary-spanning skills** as 'reticulists', a definition of which is 'people with responsibilities and skills in bridging organisational and professional boundaries'. The inter-corporate dimensions of public service planning are highly managerial and it is often up to the social worker to observe the professional playing out of these, for good or bad. Part of this skill is in **knowing where to exert pressure** when others are found wanting.

Using the **principles and skills of advocacy** a complainant must begin at the closest managerial level in the organisation, rising until you reach the level at which a response is appropriate to the challenge. Often people make the mistake of going right to the top of an organisation but your complaint is merely handed down to the point at which a junior employee cannot push it any lower. It is rather like the domino effect of being shouted at by your boss: you then shout at your staff, they go home and shout at the partner who shouts at the dog. Good reticulists will have to take action where they find services lacking in order to maintain the professionalism of both their own and the collaborative organisation because that partnership can only survive by both organisations having trust in the professional relationship with the other.

Critical practice within organisations

*Adherence to the relevant **legislation, policy and procedure** thus provides three corners of a working framework that should anchor good practice in relation to assessing and managing risk and protection. The fourth corner must be attention to **rights**.*

(Cree and Wallace in Adams et al., 2009a, p45; author's emphasis)

Cree and Wallace highlighted the importance of these four elements after a consideration of social workers failing to protect service users from risk, quoting the report of Butler-Sloss (1988) where social workers, the police and a specific paediatric consultant had not followed procedural guidelines. This resulted in unprofessional practice by all to the detriment of children and their parents.

Legislative rights

Primarily, all individuals have civil, social, political and economic rights under the Human Rights Act 1998. This came into effect in the United Kingdom on 2 October 2000 and guarantees rights under two categories. It guarantees absolute rights including freedom from torture, slavery, servitude or forced labour, and the right to a fair trial, liberty and security, etc. The second category includes limited rights that require a balance between individual and public interests. So the right to respect for private and family life is limited where behaviour is culturally considered to be unacceptable and in those cases intervention by a public body is permissible. This could occur where there is evidence of risk, abuse, criminal behaviour, or contravention of the laws of the land, for example, bigamy. However, the reasons for intervention in these cases must be justified and transparent. The Act gives five principles by which such an assessment must be judged. See **www.legislation.gov.uk/ukpga/1998/42/schedule/1** for full access to the Act.

In the final section of the report recommendations were made.

3.2 Recommendations

1. *Human rights need to be mainstreamed into the work of all those who provide relevant public services.*

2. *Human rights specific language should be used, in addition to the language of values, such as respect, fairness, and dignity, to facilitate the development of a better understanding of human rights.*

3. *Where appropriate, government departments should include human rights more explicitly in the standards applicable to public services.*

I wonder how many social workers are familiar with the actual contents of this Act? It would seem that perhaps those working with asylum seekers, victims of torture or unaccompanied or trafficked children would use this as their key legislation. However, should this not be our key lens through which to view our service users' position, especially in the cases of risk, abuse and limitations to liberty?

RESEARCH SUMMARY

Department of Health research regarding the application of the Act says:

> Our evidence to date does demonstrate that a human rights-based approach to health and social care can, and will increasingly in the future, have a tangible impact on the treatment and care of service users.

> *(Department of Health Evaluation, 2008)*

Within health provision, the Mersey Care NHS Trust, one of the participants in the Human Rights in Healthcare initiative, decided that an integral part of a human rights approach was involving service users in decisions:

> In the evaluation of service users and carers . . . we actually asked . . . has involvement, has contributing to the Trust . . . made an impact upon your recovery? And I think it was 89 per cent of service users resoundingly said yes, and not just said yes but qualified it with a raft of statements to support that: 'this has meant that

Continued

I've stayed out of hospital; this has meant that I've needed less teams treating me; this has helped me in my recovery; this has given me a life'. The actual quotations were quite moving really.

(Catherine Mills, service user and co-opted member of the Trust Board, Mersey Care NHS Trust: transcript 17.9.08)

In terms of public authorities providing services to the public, a district council in England stated that the Act had made the council 'more responsive to the public at an individual level'.

(Individual working for South Norfolk District Council and responding in a personal capacity, Call for Evidence response)

Examples cited included: positively influencing work around gypsy and traveller communities; enabling the right to family life to be balanced with the child's rights in care proceedings; and balancing privacy rights when deciding to use surveillance to tackle anti-social behaviour:

When anti-social behaviour is carried out by a handful of young people, is it fair to establish a curfew that says all young people are not allowed in certain areas after a specific time? By adding a Human Rights Act perspective . . . you can ask whether this proposed policy solution is necessary and proportionate.

(Welsh Local Government Association)

A council in Wales transformed its approach to travellers following a court case under the Human Rights Act:

It's a different way of working. Instead of being negative . . . within a week of the travellers moving on to the sites, the Council's liaison officer had been up to assess the welfare, the Local Health Board's health worker had been up to assess whether there were any health issues, and the local traveller education support worker also went up with a view of getting the children into the local schools and to sort out any educational needs which is what the Council have to do but they did it with no fuss.

(Local advice worker, North Wales Group Evidence Session)

Public sector staff can, and do, use the human rights framework in a number of ways, and their awareness of human rights is important in delivering the services that people need:

Staff awareness of human rights must be from the very moment that the customer walks through the door speaking to reception staff.

(Cllr. Lindsay Whittle, Welsh Local Government Association and Councillor, Caerphilly County Borough Council: transcript 7.10.08)

Quotes taken from the Human Rights Enquiry report accessed at www.equalityhuman rights.com

As well as this over-arching Act, there are numerous field-specific Acts to be used in the services to children, older and disabled people, those who experience mental illness and so on.

Policy and procedure

The above evidence clearly indicates that some stakeholders within health and social care had begun to change the way they operated their services following guidance on the application of new legislation. This had proved a positive experience for service users too. So how does an Act become policy in your agency and how are procedures developed to ensure that the agency is meeting its legal responsibilities?

Once an Act has obtained Royal Consent a date is set for it to come into law and guidance is given by a variety of means. This may be through special interest organisations such as Social Enterprise UK who have a network of 15,000 organisations. They are committed to raising awareness of the social value that can be added to service provision through targeted procurement and they work with local authorities and the third sector. They lobbied for the Public Services (Social Value) Act 2012 and produced guidance on its implementation with the help of solicitors (**www.cips.org**).

The Social Care Institute for Excellence has developed resources such as interactive video, publications and best practice guidance in relation to the law and social work (**www.scie.org.uk**).

The Care Quality Commission states that hospitals, care homes, dental and GP surgeries and all other care services in England should provide people with safe, effective, compassionate and high quality care, and encourages such agencies to make improvements and ensure that they are adhering to the law (**www.cqc.org.uk**).

The law relating to the care of children and young people can be found at: **www. education.gov.uk/childrenandyoungpeople/families/childrenincare**

The law relating to services for those with mental ill health can be found at: **www. gov.uk/government/organisations/department-of-health**

You see a pattern here – that the relevant departments responsible for the passage of the Act of Parliament also produce guidance; that some special interest groups act as disseminators and promoters of the Act; that regulatory bodies check services are being provided according to the law and that scholarly and research organisations ensure that evidence is gathered and offered as good practice guidance. These various levels of guidance ensure that the law is understood by professionals (the campaign for plain English was not always at home when they were compiled!); that it is put into appropriate language for service users; that evidence-based practice is gathered and used to inform 'what works'; and that service providers are monitored to make sure they comply.

Within agencies, compliance officers using all this information will work out what impact the new legislation will have on their provision, along with professionals who will engage with the continuity or change involved, and finance officers who will investigate the effectiveness, efficiency and impact incurred. At managerial levels decisions will be made as to whom to consult and in what way. In social work agencies it is common to involve service users and their carers in this process, along with an interdisciplinary approach including the private and charitable sectors.

As you can see, your agency policy has been influenced by many levels of control and by numerous discourses coming from a variety of social constructions. Often practitioners feel that in assessing someone for service provision they are assessing them out of, rather than into, receiving a service; for example, that the eligibility criteria is set to exclude people.

There is a joke in services to older people that people over 75 are eligible so long as they bring their parents (note both of them) into the assessment meeting. With predictions that increasing numbers of people born after 1980 will live to be 100 years and above, this may be a real strategy in limiting provision to increasingly scarce resourcing. Government constantly issues policy statements about social care (see **www.gov.uk/government/topics/social-care**). Currently these look at dementia care, dealing with rushed home care visits, providing extra care and support, making health and social care work together more effectively, promoting better mental well-being and accessible services. Cynically, one could look at these topics and say: 'Well of course social workers and health professionals would want to do all this but each year resources are being cut. It looks like these topics are trying to address what is going wrong with social care.'

Here is a quote from research by Jan Little into social worker definitions of their work:

> The overall emphasis on performance management, monitored by targets and performance indicators etc. serves only to separate social work from its core function: to help. In fact, a problem being masked by the plethora of performance management data is that we aren't at all clear about what we are trying to achieve by them. Performance indicators, such as how many children there are at any one time on the child protection register, are meaningless on their own. Similarly, targets are more likely to concern the completion of work within a certain time scale, rather than meeting a predetermined, highly specific and measurable outcome agreed in each individual case. For instance, all too often the 'goal' in childcare is to 'provide support', instead of 'providing support to achieve exactly what and how'.

You will be picking up these views in your placement and need to develop ways of critically analysing them rather than colluding or arguing that your colleagues are merely cynical because they have been in the work a long time. I said earlier that there were four elements to consider in a synthesis of your practice: legislation, policy, procedure and rights; the latter will now be considered. No matter what agendas insinuate themselves into social work we can always quickly locate with our original core values and beliefs when we root back to the rights agenda. It is to this we now move.

Rights

With all the organisational issues considered in this chapter it is easy to lose sight of the purpose of our work and the reasons why we became social workers and the commitment we have to alleviating discrimination and oppression. A useful way to anchor such considerations to practice is to locate them with the complexity of critical practice. I have previously written about the triumvirate of reflective, reflexive and critical practice as shown in Table 2.3.

Table 2.3   Integrating levels of critical practice

Type of practice	Function	Example
Reflective	Use after or during the event to analyse professional activity.	In supervision. During a practice session in discussion with colleagues. As part of a portfolio narrative of your practice.
Reflexive	Use before, during and/or after the event to critique the morality and virtue ethics of the event.	Respond to service users. Challenge self and others about the reasons and outcomes for/of the event.
Critical	Use before, during and after the event to critique personal and professional histories, practice and the social construction of problems.	Digest the discourse of the personal and the private, the creation of 'others' and the binaries of power that exist to discriminate and oppress.
		Disseminate your thinking through presentations, conference papers and/or publications.

At the critical stage, practice is capable of being pushed to a 'transformational' level where our experience, psychological processes, specialist knowledge, inter-subjectivity and inter-contextuality with other professionals raises our ability to set the whole context of our work within the service user context rather than the organisational one. This means that the service user and their condition are always central to our work and their rights take precedence.

ACTIVITY **2.5**

Service user rights

Molly, a 73 year old who lives alone has had a couple of falls and, according to her family, is exhibiting early signs of dementia. Her three daughters are very anxious and concerned that their mother is at serious risk of dying should she be unable to get attention if she injures herself. They have requested a visit to assess their mother for residential care and have a letter from their mother's doctor and a solicitor neighbour supporting this.

What framework might you develop to help you to focus on Molly, consider the concerns of her family and create a transformational solution to her current difficulties?

COMMENT

What is the nature of the problem and to whom? Think about the diversity, range and depth. Would it be useful to create a network map for Molly using Bronfenbrenner's systems theory, for example a diagram showing micro, meso, exo, macro and chrono levels in Molly's life as it is and how she would want it to be?

Continued

COMMENT *continued*

What other professionals would be involved/consulted? You might involve those who would counsel or advocate for Molly rather than those who might focus on the risk element and pressure from relatives.

What legislation and government guidance would inform your case for Molly to decide her own needs? You might use the Personalisation Act, the Fair Access to Care and the Human Rights Act.

What considerations would you give to the risk to your professional self if the worst were to happen to Molly and she died alone at home after a fall? How much would you need to consider the position of your agency, litigation and the influence of the press in balancing the rights and risks to all concerned?

Consider how much your practice would be a delicate balance between risk, rights, legislation, agency policy and procedure while trying to maintain some of the idealism that first prompted you to become a social worker.

CHAPTER SUMMARY

Chapter 2 has taken your placement journey into the complexity of working within organisations. The attempt was to seat your practice into the cultures, complications, contradictions and constructions of the placement experience, and into your ASYE. The importance is to realise that you are not travelling alone and need to both conform to these organisational structures yet work towards transforming them so that they serve you and your service users in enriching their lives as much as possible. It is impossible to give a fully comprehensive view of all organisations here yet some of the outlines will have posed some of the nature of their connections to policy, procedures and rights within a legislative framework. Evidence-based practice, risk and assessment documentation, multi-disciplinary practice, boundary-spanning skills and the integration of AI and EI enable social workers to occupy a unique position in pulling together creative and transformative solutions to enrich the lives of service users.

The following chapter will consolidate Chapters 1 and 2 in taking students and NQSWs through the process of becoming reflective and critical thinkers who are able to fully engage in learning opportunities, building on their attributes, university theoretical learning, and initiating opportunities for learning and development in the placement.

FURTHER
READING

Quinney, A and Hafford-Letchfield, T (2012) *Interprofessional Social Work: Effective Collaborative Approaches.* London: Sage.

This is a core book focusing on the skills needed to work across professional boundaries and with a range of different professionals. In addition to commentary on the changing landscapes of social work and a consideration of professional identities the book includes chapters on youth work, health, education, housing and social justice being the main loci of the inter-professional work of social workers.

Kline, R and Preston-Shoot, M (2012) *Professional Accountability in Social Care and Health: Challenging Unacceptable Practice and Its Management.* London: Sage.

There are numerous practice and professional activities here that will give opportunities for ethical thought for social work practitioners. Chapter 10 gives clear guidelines as to how to appropriately challenge discriminatory and oppressive practice.

USEFUL WEBSITE

www.tcsw.org.uk/uploadedFiles/TheCollege/Social_Work_Practice/RtSW%20Module%2010%20 Working%20in%20Organisations%20FINAL.pdf

Part of The College of Social Work learning materials for returning to social work professionals, this website contains many exercises and some detail of the new structures for child protection work.

Chapter 3
Embedding critical placement learning

This chapter will help you to develop the following capabilities, to the appropriate level, from the Professional Capabilities Framework:

- *Professionalism*: Describe the importance of professional behaviour; describe the importance of personal and professional boundaries.
- *Values and ethics*: Understand the profession's ethical principles and their relevance to practice.
- *Diversity*: Recognise the importance of diversity in human identity and experience, and the application of anti-discriminatory and anti-oppressive principles in social work practice.
- *Rights, justice and economic well-being*: Understand the principles of rights, justice and economic well-being, and their significance for social work practice.
- *Knowledge*: Demonstrate an initial understanding of the range of theories and models for social work intervention.
- *Critical reflection and analysis*: Recognise and describe why evidence is important in social work practice.
- *Intervention and skills*: Demonstrate awareness of a range of frameworks to assess and plan intervention. Demonstrate basic ability to produce written documents relevant for practice. Demonstrate initial awareness of risk and safeguarding.

It will also introduce you to the following standards as set out in the 2008 Social Work Subject Benchmark Statement:

4.6   Application of, and critical reflection upon, ethical principles and dilemmas.
5.1.2 The issues and trends in modern public and social policy and their relationship to contemporary practice and service delivery in social work.
5.1.3 Values and ethics relevant to the understanding and resolution of value dilemmas and conflicts in both interpersonal and professional contexts.
5.1.5 The nature of social work practice including processes that facilitate and support service user choice and independence.
5.5.4 Intervention and evaluation in undertaking practice in a manner that promotes the well-being and protects the safety of all parties.
5.9   Use ICT effectively for professional communication, data storage and retrieval and information searching.
6.2   Reflect on performance.
7.3   On graduating students should have a developed capacity for the critical evaluation of knowledge and evidence from a range of sources.

Introduction

In Chapter 1 we looked at the aims and structure of placement and some of the knowledge and skills you would need to begin the journey. This should have led to an understanding of the usefulness of creating a critical dialogue to enhance the placement experience, including how you would weave this into your planning for the placement visit.

In Chapter 2 this preparation was moved into a consideration of the placement organisation, its culture, level of job satisfaction and a variety of multi-disciplinary themes, some of which will evolve in the future to meet new needs or as a result of austerity. During this chapter some critical questions were posed for you to think about. Documentary analysis, linking purpose and function were explored and some strategies for the critical questioning of these were presented. Finally critical practice working in organisations was posed around legislation, policy, procedures and rights.

Chapter 3 moves your journey along into the critical atmosphere of the placement and illuminates the experiences you are likely to encounter. It is a world where you are both a student and a professional. You will have much to learn but also much to share from university and contribute from your own experience. You might have access to senior managers and directors of social services, a forum from which to present your ideas in team and multi-disciplinary meetings and through direct supervision to gain both affirmation and critique of your work. More of this in Chapter 4.

By the end of this chapter you will be able to:

- appreciate and use your own learning style to create a fertile learning environment in placement;

- appropriately and critically evaluate and apply theories used in social work to the placement environment;

- interpret learning opportunities using a strengths-based approach integrating attributes of emotional intelligence (EI) and appreciative inquiry (AI);

- appreciate a diversity of ideas in application to social work;

- articulate placement learning opportunities critically into placement-related academic assignments;

- recognise and refer on appropriately, behaviours that are unprofessional.

In the beginning

Congratulations, you have successfully navigated your way through the placement-finding process, presented a good image of yourself and your commitment at your informal meeting with the placement practice educator and now you have arrived at the placement agency. Wait a minute though – I hope you have done your preparation for this first day. If there was ever a time to rev your engine it is now! Some students think they can go along to their first day and place themselves in the welcoming arms of their practice educator who will then teach them everything they need to know. The essence of a good practice educator is that they know what opportunities, personnel, external agencies, legislation, policy, processes and resources to highlight for you. Only you can pursue these to extract meaningful learning to enable you to evidence your practice. This experience is so unique to each student that it is up to you to forge your specific pathway through placement.

ACTIVITY 3.1

First dates

Think about how you might prepare for the first day in placement.

What practical things would you do?

What attitude would you adopt?

How would you dress/present yourself?

COMMENT

Here are some ideas from what students have said about this.

Student A

Practically you need to take your own cup and tea bags etc., pens, notepaper, small book for reflective notes and to write questions to follow up. I always take sandwiches just in case I don't get time to go out to buy lunch. Also you get given so many papers during the first week so it is a good idea to take a ring binder. Get an A to Z of the area too. They are more useful than your phone maps because you can see the bigger picture, where the schools and leisure facilities are, hospitals, police stations for example over the whole district. Get a bus map. This will be useful for you to see what the services are like for service users as well as if you are travelling to see them by bus.

Student B

Although I was quite apprehensive on my first day I tried to be calm and smiled at people when I was introduced. I didn't initiate shaking hands though as I thought some people might prefer not to. Once my practice educator had given me some initial tasks and shown me to a desk I felt quite lost. Everyone was busy on their computers and it felt like I couldn't interrupt them. When I noticed some of the staff going for refreshments I went too. I introduced myself to them, told them where I was from and that I would be working with them for six months. At least it felt like I had a group I could say hello to each morning. I read the notices in the office and picked up some of the leaflets there to familiarise myself with current information. Then I went to look at the signing-out system and checked with the office that I had understood the system correctly. When I could get on a computer I began checking the legislation and policy guidance under which the service operated. This was really useful as I had forgotten quite a lot since studying it at uni.

Continued

Student C

During the first week of my placement I checked it was ok for me to do a brief community audit. I bought the local paper, visited the health centre, library, civic centre, and one or two of the voluntary organisations based in the town centre. I went round the shops and the market. I noticed that there was a small Marks and Spencer store but that the main post office, MacDonalds and Mothercare had closed. There were lots of pound shops and numerous betting shops, payday loans shops and charity shops. I logged my observations in my reflective log book.

Student D

I had asked about the dress code at my pre-placement meeting and was told it was smart/casual. I wasn't sure if I could wear nice jeans so I didn't and was glad as when I arrived I saw that the staff had casual trousers and jackets/tops. I had taken my earrings out but saw that it was ok to wear jewellery. Some staff also wore quite heavy makeup.

As you can see, these students had begun their placement by applying curiosity, taking responsibility for their own learning and judging how to fit in with their agency norms.

People who will support your learning while in placement

You will appreciate that you are not expected to know everything about practice when you begin your placement. However, you are expected to know about theory, research, legislation (generally), how to communicate and how to acknowledge differing report types and assessment pro formas. These topics will have comprised part of your learning while in university.

Here are some of the sources of support to begin your practice development.

Personnel

- practice educator (on- or off-site);
- agency supervisor (if you have an off-site practice educator);
- agency teams;
- tutor;
- multi-disciplinary teams within or outside your agency;
- other students, either in the agency or part of your course cohort;
- service users and their carers;
- university counsellor (university recall days).

Documentation

- agency directories;

- annual reports;

- operating policy guidance, e.g. community care plans, child protection reports;

- reports from national bodies about the agency, e.g. Ofsted;

- serious case reviews relating to practice within the agency or other local involvement;

- good practice guidelines, e.g. from SCIE relating to your agency practice.

In the first days of the placement your practice educator will cover the following with you:

- An induction to include relevant documentation, e.g. health and safety, lone working policy, office protocol.

- Introduction to the staff group to include your workspace, office security, shadowing procedures, the range of work you will be expected to gradually take on.

- Supervision arrangements and agreement regarding how this will be managed, e.g. what will be expected of whom in these regular meetings.

- Guidance as to what to do if you are unsure, anxious or worried about how to proceed. This may include who to talk to if you encounter poor or discriminatory practice or if a complaint is made against you.

- What the process will be in the event of failing to meet the key roles or HCPC standards.

Although these last two elements can be daunting, it is important that any lack of opportunity to practise or student inability to provide evidence should be picked up at the earliest moment so that plans can be made to reverse the situation. As a student, other members of staff will be asked about how you are practising, for example, how you fit in with the team, how you use resources and about your general skills in communication and professional behaviour. It is a useful mantra to imagine how you are demonstrating professional behaviour even when you are not being observed.

Activity 3.2 shows an example of a placement that initially seemed to lack opportunities for the student to gather critical evidence for his portfolio.

ACTIVITY **3.2**

Jack's placement

Jack was placed in a voluntary organisation working with young people who had learning disabilities within a short-term residential unit. Although the organisation was part of a larger sister unit, the unit within which Jack was placed had only a small number

Continued

of residential support workers who tended to go with the residents to community activities during the day. He became increasingly frustrated, perceiving that he did not have any 'proper social work' to get his teeth into and was anxious that he would not be able to provide evidence for the successful completion of the key roles. A meeting was held between Jack, his practice educator and tutor to plan the way forward.

What strategies might Jack use to plan how he would develop work sufficient to evidence his key roles?

What elements of critical thinking would help with this activity?

COMMENT

Both Jack and the agency were focusing on the work that the agency currently did with service users. This meant that they were trying to identify key role opportunities within that work. Once they began to look at Jack's role as 'developmental' he was linked into the agency's broader service provision which opened up a more critical debate about the practice of the agency and his role within it. Following this he began to create links with external agencies, and set up meetings with carers and families to plan more imaginative ways to enhance service users' time with them. He completed risk analyses to enable a greater community presence for the service users and the agency.

Through shifting Jack's anxiety from evidencing the key roles to developing his skills in criticality, networking and exploring a social justice approach to inclusion, Jack and the agency were able to refocus the work and to allow him to enjoy the placement.

Creating your own fertile learning environment in placement

We might be aware of the conditions under which we learn best, but might not have formally analysed these. It is simple when using self-directed learning to use the learning systems that are most effective for ourselves. When we have to conquer a new skill we might:

- get a book on how to do it, e.g. make a cake, build a dry stone wall;

- ask someone how to do it, e.g. change the pressure in a combi-boiler;

- watch someone doing it, e.g. sew a zip in a garment, knead bread;

- look on the internet, e.g. YouTube, websites;

- have a go and learn from our mistakes, e.g. change a tyre, cure a leak;

- any other ways you have used . . . these are just my ways!

In placement you will have limited time to learn and the quicker you can show your practice educator your style of learning the quicker you will achieve. One way to do this is to complete a SWOT analysis of your learning. This acronym represents Strengths, Weaknesses, Opportunities and Threats and is usually represented as shown in Figure 3.1.

Strengths	Weaknesses
I don't panic but think about how to react carefully and calmly.	I like to be in control and don't react well if I feel I don't have the knowledge.
I am confident in new situations.	I struggle with conflict.
I am very practical and like to work hard.	I get tired easily and frustrated if I can't achieve my best.
Opportunities	**Threats**
I want to develop my ability to do complex risk assessments.	I'm afraid I will be embarrassed because my experience will be out of date.
I would like to learn how to present cases in formal meetings.	I am unsure how to handle silences.
I would like to learn strategies for working under pressure.	I am terrified of going to present at court.

Figure 3.1   Using a SWOT analysis

ACTIVITY **3.3**

Critical thinking and your SWOT analysis

Add your own comments to each of the four areas to encapsulate evidence of your own critical thinking.

COMMENT

This is not so hard to do and will get you in the habit of always thinking about critical practice.

Strengths *– Think about how you bring in ideas of social justice to your practice and through this are able to see how service users are socially constructed. This means you are aware that in the wider world outside your office, service users are discriminated against because of who they are, what they look like, how they present and the fact that they are different from the so-called norm. This 'difference' poses a threat to others who are ignorant of the difficulties experienced by your service users.*

So you might write: 'I know that through my core values and beliefs I strive to work in ways that help to balance the injustice my service users experience in their worlds.'

Continued

COMMENT *continued*

Weaknessess – *Think about how difficult it might be for you to use power and control in situations that demand it. This might mean that you fail to recognise and use legitimate power and control in situations that might leave service users at risk. This is risky practice for the placement agency as they will be held accountable should something occur because you have not taken action.*

So you might write: 'I am anxious that I may fail to use power and control legitimately and a mishap may occur that causes me to embarrass the agency and that may result in harm to a service user.'

Opportunities – *Think beyond the descriptive nature of the placement agency to the philosophy (often they will have a mission statement), policies and procedures. The public statements issued by the agency are often 'hearts and flowers', meaning they profess a very benign view for service users. The operational policies and procedures, on the other hand, function to define eligibility criteria that exclude people in order to meet limited budgets, and the procedures might be 'tick box' and risk averse.*

So you might write: 'I would welcome the opportunity to learn about the management agendas and explore some of the mechanisms for the deployment of government initiatives and staff feedback.'

Threats – *Think about what you have heard about high caseloads once qualified. You might be wondering what the norms are for this and feel that, in order to test your ability to manage and prioritise a caseload, you will be put under pressure. You are worried about this in light of the amount of work you have to do on your university degree.*

So you might write: 'Although I know that I must be tested working under pressure I would like some guidance as to who I talk to about this.'

Hold the idea of this SWOT analysis with critical thinking and remember to complete one for yourself ready to use in your first supervision session with your practice educator. You might also be asked to complete other types of learning styles questionnaires that your practice educator finds useful.

Using theory and critical thinking in your placement practice

There have, historically, been numerous arguments about whether social work is a true profession, the definition of which is:

> *Occupation, practice, or vocation requiring mastery of a complex set of knowledge and skills through formal education and/or practical experience. Every organised profession (accounting, law, medicine, etc.) is governed by its respective professional body.*

> (www.businessdictionary.com/definition/profession.html#ixzz2wWBMB64M)

Initially, the professions were seen as medicine, the law and religion but now these have somewhat widened and one can use the term 'professional builder' and 'professional footballer'. However, the same principles as stated above apply. There is an imperative to behave in an honest, moral way and to conform to the ethical standards and rules of the profession.

Other terms now adhere to the definition of a profession, for example that members participate in continuing professional development (CPD). It is clear that the set of knowledge and skills referred to in the above definition is specific to that profession.

Yet social work applies theoretical constructions from a range of other professions, for example, systems theory from biology; psychodynamic, crisis intervention, cognitive behavioural and solution-focused theory from psychology; risk assessment from clinical practice; and anti-oppressive and anti-discriminatory approaches from equality and human rights discourses. Additionally, some of the theories have evolved to refer to social work specifically, such as task-centred practice and social group work first used in America to deal with a shortage of social workers and high client needs.

This eclecticism is the social workers' professional armour, enabling us to integrate a variety of theories, methods, strategies, frameworks and models to best meet the breadth of service user, carer, agency and governmental needs in a post-modern society. So we may conclude that although social work is a profession it does not hold a unique set of theory applicable only to itself. It is in this flexibility that social work celebrates the ability to acquire and jettison theory in response to the shifting and contested nature of social work.

Additionally, as stated above, theory is played out through the use of methods, strategies, frameworks and models. Here are a few; by no means a comprehensive list but enough to give you some idea of the complexity.

Theories to help us understand the individual or situation

I have included some links here to help you with some preliminary research but these are by no means a replacement for reading original texts or collective critical texts that give you comparisons of theories used in social work. One of these is Malcolm Payne's (2005) *Modern Social Work Theory*. Not all ways of working are included here as some lend themselves to very specific practices.

Attachment: **http://eyfs.info/articles/_/child-development/attachment-theory-and-the-key-person-approach-r64**

Psychodynamic: **http://gaps.org.uk/sites/default/files/Using%20psychodynamic%20perspectives%20in%20social%20work%20cprc%20FINAL%202012–1.pdf**

Systems and ecological and social learning theory: **www.jstor.org/stable/10.1086/341185?__redirected**

Humanism: **www.youtube.com/watch?v=84POCehz3xk**

Cognitive, behavioural: **www.youtube.com/watch?v=eGr2KQy8ypE**

Maslow's Hierarchy of Needs: **http://timvandevall.com/printable-maslows-hierarchy-of-needs-chart**

Eriksson's 7 stages: **www.journal.kfionline.org/issue-6/erik-eriksons-theory-of-development-a-teachers-observations**

Grief and loss: **www.slideshare.net/Shallon_Hylton/grief-and-loss-12997650**

Prochaska and DiClemente – cycle of change: **www.addictioninfo.org/articles/11/1/Stages-of-Change-Model/Page1.html**

Communication as practice: **www.scie.org.uk/publications/guides/guide05 appendixb.asp**

Social constructionism and discourse analysis: **www1.uwindsor.ca/criticalsocialwork/discourse-analysis-in-critical-social-work-from-apology-to-question**

Multi-disciplinary work: **www.youtube.com/watch?v=Fh7tlr4Tl1o**

Methods

The methods chosen will reflect the theory(ies) used. These may be based on talking therapies, scientifically calculated projections, future basing intentions and wishes, analyses of role transactions, notions of the impact of environment and history, beliefs in the individual's ability to heal, the collective responses across multi-professional teams, and so on. For example, in using a systems approach, a social worker might use a 'network map' to assess how a person sees themselves in relation to their environment. This can be used over time to reflect progression/regression. Supporting the creation of the network map the social worker will use motivational cues, listen and communicate effectively and engage with the implications of the map.

Here are some other methods applied in social work:

- questioning, exchange, procedural, actuarial, clinical, risk assessments;
- motivational interviewing technique;
- skilled helper;
- psychoanalytical;
- risk assessment;
- therapeutic relationship;
- listening;
- communication and engagement;
- empathy;
- multi-disciplinary working partnerships.

Strategies

The strategies used to carry out the methods will also relate to the theory. For example, using a network map, a social worker will use evaluation to interpret the meaning for the service user.

- evaluation;

- empowerment;

- advocacy;

- user involvement;

- supervision and development;

- working in partnership;

- reflective, reflexive and critical practice.

Frameworks

Those generated by the theories will be used to establish how the work will be framed and evaluated, for example, the types of activities and purpose of the work and how it will be interpreted with the service user. Using the same example of the network map, a service user may indicate which situations lead to substance misuse and using the 12-step recovery framework the worker will be able to interpret relapse as part of that process rather than as failure.

- life stages and stages of interventions;

- cycles of repair and relapse;

- processes leading to critical thinking.

Models

Models will help the social worker to professionalise how they reflect upon and interpret their work with service users. For example, using the network map idea again, the social worker will be intellectually engaged with a range of models that give substance and accountability to practice. This is so that gut feeling, intuition, personal experiences and the 'sitting by Nellie approach' do not govern the sensitive nature of the social worker's interpretation of their service user's situation.

- reflection;

- transactional analysis;

- evaluation;

- solution-focused and narrative;

- person-centred;

- advocacy;

- group work;

- counselling;

- attachment and loss;

- cognitive/behavioural;

- behavioural;

- psychodynamic;

- crisis intervention;

- social learning;

- task-centred.

I have attempted to separate these titles into the five areas of theories, methods, strategies, frameworks and models to enable you to see that doing social work is a highly complex task and it is not sufficient to say you are using, say, one theory. You also need to know how to practise using that theory and what the implications are for the service user. This is rather like shopping for an important item. You need to know what the alternatives are, is the price right, is it the best deal you can achieve, how might you feel about it in the future, is it right for you and are you convinced it will add to the contentment of your life?

In appropriately and critically evaluating a complex mesh of these attributes you will begin to see the intellectual challenge you need to meet in order to provide the best possible practice to your service users and their carers.

So far in this chapter I have laid out the ground level of thinking into practice. However, to be a truly critical practitioner takes more than this. Let us take a few examples of how other authors have explained critical practice.

Adams, Dominelli and Payne entitled their first chapter 'On being critical in social work' (Adams et al., 2009b, pp 1–14). It is worth reading this now. Essentially, they view 'being critical' as thinking and acting through using our judgement about oppression, diversity, through taking the viewpoint of the vulnerable, giving voice to the seldom heard, and by working this through to an evaluation of its impact on services and striving to change them.

In my book *Critical Learning for Social Work Students* (Jones, 2013), I set down some action points to sensitise you to learning to be a critical practitioner. These were: to be careful about misusing your power; to check that you do not misunderstand key issues of discrimination and oppression; and to be careful that you have not failed to recognise significant events and consequently failed to take action.

To help you to avoid these errors I said you must: critique, analyse, evaluate, synthesise and reframe your perspectives.

The challenges that face you in doing so are: discerning what are the dilemmas and tensions, how you deal with unknowing and uncertainty and the emotional confusion that comes with the complexity of elation or despair (Jones, 2013, pp4–5).

One of the most useful texts in this area, at least for me, has been Jan Fook's (2002) book *Social Work: Critical Theory and Practice*. Originally written in 2002, it presents a clear exposition of the theory, skills, strategies, methods and models of critical social work practice. Fook interweaves a comprehensive and dense cloth of discourse analysis, social constructionism, narrative, oppositional thinking, ways of knowing and unknowing, critical resistance and change, reconstruction, politicisation, resistance and challenge.

In their 'concluding comments' in *Practising Social Work in a Complex World* (2009c, pp331–55), Adams et al. state that 'critical practice is transformational' (p334). It is inherently the transposition of morality into action. This is a view also taken by Barnett (1997) in the development of his criticality framework that informed research by the ESRC into the teaching and learning of criticality in social work. It was conducted under the auspices of Southampton University by Johnston et al. and presented at the 6th Joint Social Work Education Conference in 2004.

Table 3.1 guides the reader through four levels of criticality moving through the three domains of knowledge, self and the world.

Table 3.1   Levels, domains and forms of critical being

	Domains		
Levels of criticality	**Knowledge**	**Self**	**World**
4 Transformatory critique	Knowledge critique	Reconstruction of self	Critique-in-action (collective reconstruction) of the world
3 Refashioning of traditions	Critical thought (malleable traditions of thought)	Development of self within traditions	Mutual understanding and development of traditions
2 Reflexivity	Critical thinking (reflection on one's understanding)	Self-reflection (reflection on one's own projects)	Reflective practice (meta-competence, adaptability, flexibility)
1 Critical skills	Discipline, specific critical thinking skills	Self-monitoring to give standards and norms	Problem-solving (means–end instrumentalism)

Source: Barnett (1997).

Essentially, Barnett was concerned with the lack of clear definitions of criticality and the sense that reflective thinking, knowledge, skills and professionalism and the links between formal and informal knowledge, the self and action, were, in their consummate parts the elements constituting critical thinking. Rather like the sum of the working body being more than a collection of its parts, critical thinking is often identified by a balance of deep and connected analysis situated within a discipline context and bringing to bear the mastery of self-knowledge and world appreciation. It is rather like 'I know it when I see it', yet it is as if the sprinkling of some magical dust occurs to fuse these elements together at some moment in time, creating that thing we call 'criticality'. Magical thinking is present causing something like the synapses to spark in unison just at the right time to produce some eureka event that boosts our levels of understanding. The trick then is in how to harness this sort of thinking in preparing for the placement, and beyond.

Let us practise Barnett's second level of criticality – that of reflexivity.

ACTIVITY **3.4**

Using Barnett's criticality framework to prepare for placement: reflexive skills

Using the descriptors for level 2 reflexivity, think about how you might prepare for practice.

Critical thinking and reflecting on your understanding

How can you optimise your understanding of theory used in social work?

(You might choose a theory you are familiar or comfortable with and create some critical questions while doing further reading about it. How much does task-centred theory address anti-discriminatory issues?)

Self-reflection on your own projects

What skills in self-critical analysis would enable you to excavate your true abilities and prejudices and develop strategies to work with them?

(What are your true thoughts, values and beliefs about service users, including those who are difficult to help or who are involuntary? What skills and strategies do you need to develop to encompass the ethical values of social work in these cases?)

Reflective practice and the use of meta-competence, adaptability and flexibility

How might you move your reflective skills into reflexive skills through which you embrace the higher order abilities which have to do with being able to learn (rather than being taught), adapt, anticipate and create and to use judgement, intuition, adaptability, flexibility and acumen?

(How might you translate this paragraph into a more global understanding of the people you work with in order to understand the discourse and social constructions that impact on their lives?)

COMMENT

First, it is important to say that the methods of working with people, for example, task-centred, psychodynamic systems theories, have evolved from the creation of scientific thinkers who all held particular values and beliefs about the efficacy of their theory. Most were European white males from the higher-educated classes who were not disabled or openly gay, from a minority ethnic group or aged. Second, theories of culture, philosophy, human rights, power, political orientation, discourse and social constructionism must form

COMMENT *continued*

*part of the social work students' **knowledge repertoire** if they are to become critical and reflexive practitioners. This shifts the emphasis of practice from a certainty that some absolute truth or correct way exists, to the power of the narrative of the lived experience, particularly of service users, but also of the practitioner as actor within the caring professions. There are a number of texts on **critical social work practice** and you should read through these prior to going on placement. I have listed two at the end of this chapter.*

Deepening critical reflection

There are a huge number of theorists and texts imploring all types of practitioners **towards critical self-reflection**. Why is this and of what importance is it for you? In a shifting and uncertain world there is less comfort to be gained in the sustained order of things. Post-modernity means a greater emphasis on interpreting the world through how the actors see it and not because of a certainty in the continuation of the old order. The name of the game is change and change again as we see in educational institutions, government policies, social resourcing (or not), levels of policing, civil servants and health services. This is unsettling if we are unable to make sense of it for both ourselves and those we serve. Developing a narrative of our understanding through **anticipatory and contemplative dialogues** leads us to an appreciative position from which we are able to create order from chaos and where action becomes clear. You might say you already reflect, you do not see it as important, you have not got the time, it is navel gazing, you need to get on with the task. It is true that to some extent social work has become outcome related, functionalist, means-to-an-end work. This is what has caused the serious events that blight the name of social work. With the reframing of social work through The College of Social Work and the recommendations from SCRs, part of your 'mission' is to ensure that you take the art of critical self-reflection into the **domain of reflexivity**. After reading about skills used in reflexivity, think about how you can evidence these. You might choose to adopt new ways of thinking, challenge your beliefs, examine where your values come from, think about what effect your attending university has on those close to you, decide what to jettison, open up your ideas to critique (from those who do not think as you do), discuss dilemmas with a critical friend, position yourself in the world and take responsibility for understanding why things are as they are. Seek out knowledge, marshal evidence and respond to injustice and the oppressive and discriminatory practice of others. It is not easy but if you use these drivers you will be well equipped when you begin placement.

Meta-competence simply means the ability to go the extra mile in your practice. A competence in professional practice is a functionalist, outcome-based statement about behaviour that can be observed in practice. A deep, rather than surface level, approach that evidenced meta-competence would be one that considered how, why, what, when and who might have some influence in the construction of why the competence needs to be performed. Why at that time and for that person and by you as the practitioner? Your engagement with reflexivity should cause you to seek avenues of learning through using **intuition, judgement, anticipation and contemplative thinking**. You should develop an attitude of feeling that there is always more to learn on a topic, approach this flexibly, adapt to new ideas and use your acumen in seeing connections between ideas. This is the creativity of professional artistry that replaces the technical rationality of doing just enough to meet the levels of professional standards. You might think about what type of service users use the placement, why they are there and why they are not able to solve their problems. You should think about what effect using the placement agency would have on them, who has made decisions about what the agency should provide and what views the media, research, the general population and government have about these service users. Do not forget to situate yourself as a worker within your analysis and to examine whether there are cultural dimensions that differ.

These 'ways of being' in the placement, attitudes and dispositions of mind will steer you towards a deep and critical appreciation of how your practice should be constantly evolving. You will need to take responsibility for its ongoing development throughout your career.

Developing learning opportunities to support your critical development

In this chapter you have experienced some of the debates about the complexity of social work. However, it is important that you are able to see those within the whole field of what social work is. This means to seat yourself in the middle of how you need to develop your self-awareness, qualities and attributes, political and social analysis, knowledge and skills repertoire, learning style, and practise all of this within the context of your placement, the organisation, cultural diversity and the society within which it takes place. Some might say that you need an awareness of global social politics too, especially with respect to immigration policies, internecine wars and the legal status of those who are gay, women, disabled or older.

It will be useful here to look at the entire aspect of the student social worker, you, within the embrace of the Panoptican of Social Work (see Figure 3.2).

As you can see, there will be no shortage of opportunities to further your learning in any of these fields. Additionally, you will be framing your learning around the key roles and the HCPC guidance on standards of conduct, performance and ethics in practice. It is important here to say that you should be appreciating all aspects of the cases you are working with and sequentially drawing out those areas of evidence that fulfil your key roles and HCPC, rather than focusing only on those latter areas needed as evidence to present in your practice portfolio. Such a holistic approach will allow you to relax into your work rather than taking piecemeal elements as evidence.

The Panoptican has highlighted six areas within which you can pursue your specific learning opportunities.

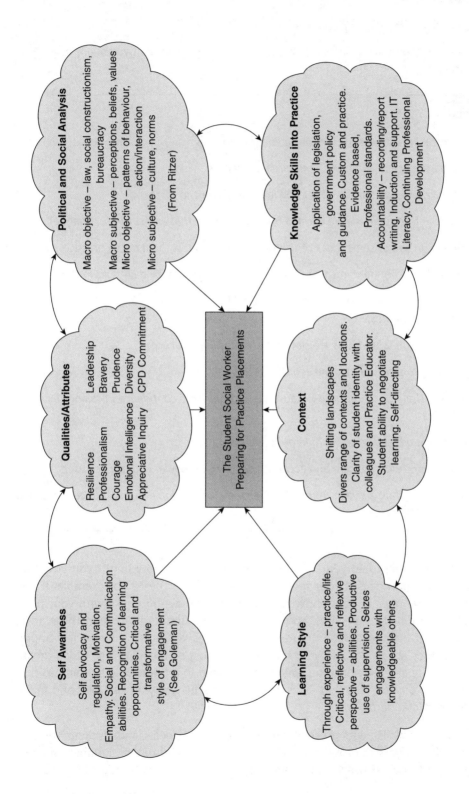

Figure 3.2   The Panoptican of Social Work

ACTIVITY **3.5**

My learning opportunities in placement

From each of the six areas highlight at least two learning needs that you might have while on placement.

COMMENT

There may be several reasons for your choices as follows:

1. *you have a personal interest in an area of practice;*

2. *you acknowledge gaps in your knowledge and want to fill them;*

3. *you have received negative critique and want to use that as a driver for change;*

4. *you are unsure of some areas of theory and want to test them out in practice;*

5. *you feel less confident in some areas of practice and want to gain skills in them;*

6. *you want to acquire skills ready for your ASYE such as chairing, commissioning or planning attributes;*

7. *you are unsure about how legislation translates into practice;*

8. *you want to start doing some action research;*

9. *you are afraid of doing duty because you do not have confidence in taking decisions in a crisis;*

10. *you find it difficult to speak in large meetings;*

11. *you struggle with the care and control ideas of using power with service users;*

12. *you feel culturally naive as you have no experience of people from other cultures; and so on . . .*

Now you have identified your 12 areas for development how might you structure your learning journey and your feelings connected with these? For example, if you know you have gaps in your knowledge you need to identify these with your practice educator/on-site supervisor. You might feel excited about pursuing these areas or reluctant if they have been pointed out to you as lacking. You might feel apprehensive if they are to do with your misunderstanding of theory or use of legitimate power. Despite any reluctance on your part you need to reframe your learning so that it is seen as a positive step that takes you towards achieving your key roles and fulfilling the HCPC standards.

Generally most placements proceed without cause for concern and students successfully develop drivers to grow as learning practitioners and gather suitable evidence for their portfolios. However, there are some who struggle with adult learning and focus on what blocks their learning. These students are often concerned with their own needs as learners and lack focus on their responsibility for self-critique and active engagement in seeking out learning opportunities.

Look at the following scenarios and decide what action you think the students should take in order to demonstrate their critical learning abilities.

ACTIVITY 3.6

Demonstrating critical learning abilities in the placement

1. *I wanted to learn more about systems theory in practice but my placement agency doesn't do it.*

2. *My first supervision session did not go well as I was late and had forgotten to bring my practice handbook. I felt the practice educator was over critical of me and that she doesn't like me.*

3. *I have a very good relationship with one of the mums I am working with but my practice educator says I need to be more focused on the care of the children and take action if necessary.*

4. *The feedback from one of my direct observations was very adversely critical and now I feel I cannot trust my practice educator if I admit to doing something wrong.*

5. *I volunteered to be part of writing a contract for commissioning a service for the agency but my practice educator said it was not appropriate.*

6. *I had an upsetting phone call on my mobile while out on a visit and so I went home. Now my practice educator wants me to see her about it.*

7. *I had an idea about developing some group work around craft skills but the agency is reluctant to do it because it is not what they usually do.*

8. *The agency does not seem to be able to provide me with opportunities to evidence my key roles and the HCPC.*

9. *I have been asked to establish contact with local community leaders but I have no idea how to go about this or even if they will accept a female student.*

10. *I have been asked to present some small training exercise to the staff group but I am terrified of doing it and will go off sick if I am made to do it.*

COMMENT

In all the above the first step is to ask yourself some critical questions. In (1) the agency may well not currently use systems theory but think about why this might be. What might be a rationale for trialling it and what might the consequences be for all stakeholders? In

Continued

(2) one can feel the sense of annoyance from a busy practice educator who has blocked time for your supervision session. You need to claim your lack of responsibility and pre-paredness. By using EI you should be able to see that your behaviour and thoughts are unprofessional and you need to be contrite and apologise, making sure it does not hap-pen again. Point (3) shows how you can be seduced into warm feelings of having good relationships with this mum. Stand back and think why she is drawing you into a 'friend-ship' relationship when having a social worker intervene into her child rearing is not the most obvious friend one would choose? What is your remit for working with her? What are the consequences for your relationship should you have to take legitimate action to protect her child and how would you deal with this? Remember, practice educators are highly experienced.

Reflect on feedback from your observation in (4) and write down why you feel it was overly critical then discuss this with the observer. Be honest but professional and claim the feelings you have while stating that you feel a loss of openness between you. Stress that you want to learn from the experience and consider it a driver for change. Ask your-self why you thought it was acceptable to volunteer for a high profile task such as in (5). Why did you not put this first to your practice educator who would probably say that you had not developed the necessary knowledge and skills at this point? You may have high ambitions for your practice but learn to walk before you try to run. Putting you in such a situation could have exposed your deficiencies and led to a bad and damaging experience for you. When you are on placement you behave as if working and therefore you must not use your private mobile phone as in (6) unless there are exceptional circumstances that must be agreed by the practice educator. Where circumstances cause you to use the 'flight' reaction, going home without notifying anyone, ringing in sick when you are not sick, to cope with an upsetting event is unprofessional. Further the situation is worsened as you are now expecting a telling off and go to the meeting with your practice educator in a defensive state where you may 'fight' your corner and make matters worse.

In (7) you need to think through the consequences of opening up new opportunities that the agency would be unable to offer once you have left. How might the activity be used to train service users to continue or the work be defined as a short-term intensive activity only but perhaps used to generate material for a bidding contract to draw in resources for the future? All agencies offering student placements have been validated to ensure there are learning opportunities commensurate with the key roles and HCPC standards so (8) seems to show that the student is passive in identifying what these are for her/ him. Creativity is the essence of social work and so you need to think of alternative ways of working. These might be exploring sister organisations, using your practice educator's links to supporting services, and introducing new theories, skills and strategies into their practice.

It is always difficult to imagine working with other cultures as in (9) when you have no experience of them. Do your research, check out minority services and personnel in the

Continued

COMMENT *continued*

area and go with an open mind. What can you and your service offer them, how would they prefer you to work with them, how might your agency adapt to be more inclusive? Develop questions that demonstrate your willingness to collaborate and read up on how minority ethnic service users experience discrimination and oppression from mainline provision. Most people, if honest, would admit to being terrified of presenting some staff training as in (10). What critical questions might you ask about this? Why are you afraid of speaking in public, are you sure of the subject matter? How can you make the experience collaborative rather than you speaking all the time? Think about how you learn, mostly through doing some activity rather than listening for lengthy periods.

Creating your own critical learning questions while in placement

Fundamentally, a critical practitioner will always begin by applying questioning techniques around ideology and consequently discourse and social constructionism.

PRACTICE LEARNING EXAMPLES

A good example of this is the dichotomy between the social and medical models of thinking about being supported to have a bath. Yes, criticality can be applied to quite low order activities! A 'medical' bath would encompass elements of health safety, the need to conform to cleanliness and social norms of acceptability. A 'social' bath would take in the potential bather's desire for a bath based on their usual practice, their views of social acceptability and upbringing. One older woman said to me quite proudly that she had a bath once a month whether she needed it or not. Yet we see that care standards in residential care set standards and targets for such matters and those residents who refuse to conform are seen as troublesome.

In developing critical questions to yourself you would begin by looking at **whether** the service user is content with how they live and how the provision from your agency could enhance this? **How** might the agency policies, rules and procedures impact on the person's life in both positive and negative ways? What are the **implications** for the applied risk analysis and how will the tensions and dilemmas that this creates be managed by you and the agency?

Beginning your critical questioning in this way means that you expose the **true/false** nature of your own discourse and social construction of the service user and how they are perceived by the agency. The next phase is to think about how they are **perceived in society**. The discourse on older people is complex as the young/old and the old/old have very differing needs.

73

PRACTICE LEARNING EXAMPLE

1. An older woman's view

When asked about why older people seem to look much younger these days, one woman told me that it was because they have benefitted from better health provision, have looked after themselves, had technological devices to take the strain out of running a home and raising children and have an expectation of being active for longer. In short she said we believe we should take responsibility for our health and well-being and in the rights that older people have. She expressed a greater confidence in speaking about her rights as an older woman. She will therefore have greater expectations about how she will be treated when she needs service provision.

2. Student realisation

A student mentioned that she had a salutary experience when working with an older man. She had a good relationship with her grandfather, who was rather deaf, and everyone in her family tended to shout when speaking to him. He missed a lot and they had begun to treat him in a rather childlike way. On one visit she realised that she was talking to the service user like she spoke to her grandfather and immediately lowered her voice and tone. He smiled and remarked that they would get on better now she had started to speak to him properly. This eureka moment made her realise that she needed to develop a more professional and contemplative approach.

Fook (2002) refers to this latter example as '**dualism**', the difference between experience and the ability/awareness to act upon it; the difference between consciousness and changed action that is core to critical practice.

Concomitant to such criticality for most of us is the need to work across multi-ethnic communities, with gender and ability differences and with age and sexuality and class that pose different spheres of **lived experiences and knowledge** with which we are unfamiliar. The societal discourses and social constructions of these groups often exist within the different arenas of the state and law, social policy and governance, agency policies and procedures, local communities and special interest groups, communities of practice, sociological groupings and the family and individuals. Do you see that I have expressed that as a **hierarchy of power**? I could equally have written the list back to front with the individual's interpretation of their own discourse coming first. Which of course it should be, but how often does the direction of influence emanate from the most powerful rather than the oppressed? Fook (2002, p61) describes this '**directionality**' as 'in favour of some, not of others'.

In using skills in one area you unintentionally discriminate against others. For example, the student above used her experience in talking with the grandfather but this method was totally inappropriate for her work with an older service user who was not deaf. Her motivation was intentionally good yet alienating because she had not critically questioned herself about how she should practise with an older male service user. Had he been blind, or black or upper class or gay she would have needed to examine her communication techniques and knowledge areas in much greater reflexive detail. By the way, have you remembered the difference between 'reflective' and 'reflexive'? The latter implies reflection plus, resulting in a changed position and practice, due to a new understanding of action.

Finally these are just a few of the words, taken from above, that could form part of your critical questions framework in practice: whether, how, implications, true/false, agency impact, societal perceptions, dualism, lived experiences and knowledge, hierarchy of power and directionality. Were you to use these in your reflective log you would surely impress your practice educator!

CHAPTER SUMMARY

Chapter 3 has given you some examples of the thick contextual mesh that you will need to create in order to embed your practice as a truly critical social worker. There are frameworks to support and guide you through the process of building upon your scaffold of knowledge. You may find or create frameworks that are more useful to you, but it is essential that you are grounded in some accountable ways of working so you are able to justify your thinking and actions when required. That is not to say that you cannot use your creativity but that you do not lurch from gut reaction to personal experience only. The PCF elements of Professionalism, Values, Diversity, Rights, Knowledge, Critical Reflection and Intervention and Skills have been integrated into the various activities and practice examples, but it is your synthesis of all this that will propel you through the placement and into your ASYE. These critical skills will be moved forward through Chapter 4 – Preparing for and using supervision.

FURTHER READING

Adams, R, Dominelli, L and Payne, M (2009) *Critical Practice in Social Work*, 2nd edition. Basingstoke: Palgrave Macmillan.

Chapter 1 provides some of the foundation for a grounding in criticality and critical thinking in social work. There is a useful practice example and some deconstruction of appropriate theories use in critical thinking. The term 'reflexivity' is also applied to learning around a narrative approach.

Fook, J (2002) *Social Work: Critical Theory and Practice*. London: Sage.

I would suggest you buy this book and dip into it. Jan Fook takes us on an easily understandable journey through some complex issues with clear case studies and well-explained narratives on discourse, critical deconstruction and reconstruction. Do not be put off by those terms any more; just read Chapter 7 in this book.

USEFUL WEBSITES

www.youtube.com/watch?v=84POCehz3xk

There is always something wonderful about using TV as a learning tool and this 18-minute clip from Frank Furedi on the nature of humanism is no exception. Watch and enjoy, it is highly relevant to all aspects of critical social work practice.

Chapter 4

Preparing for and using supervision

This chapter will help you to develop the following capabilities, to the appropriate level, from the Professional Capabilities Framework:

- *Professionalism*: Describe the mutual roles and responsibilities in supervision; describe the importance of emotional resilience in social work.
- *Values and ethics*: Demonstrate awareness of own personal values and how these can impact on practice.
- *Critical reflection and analysis*: Understand the role of reflective practice and demonstrate basic skills of reflection.
- *Intervention and skills*: Demonstrate core communication skills and the capacity to develop them.
- *Contexts and organisations*: Demonstrate awareness of the importance of professional leadership in social work (this relates to an awareness of the role and purpose of leadership within the supervisory relationship).

It will also introduce you to the following standards as set out in the 2008 Social Work Subject Benchmark Statement:

4.7   Acquire and apply the habits of critical reflection, self-evaluation and consultation.

5.1.3 The complex relationships between justice, care and control in social welfare and the practical and ethical implications of these, including roles as statutory agents and in upholding the law in respect of discrimination.

5.3   Understand the significance of the concepts of continuing professional development and lifelong learning, and accept responsibility for their own continuing development.

5.5.3 Analyse and synthesise knowledge gathered for problem-solving purposes.

5.8   Reflect on and modify behaviour in the light of experience.

6.2   Practice and skills experience – processes in which a student learns practice skills and applies theoretical models and research evidence together with new understanding to relevant activities, and receives feedback from various sources on performance, enhancing openness to critical self-evaluation.

Introduction

Chapter 2, which looked at an organisational journey and Chapter 3, which examined embedding critical learning, have given you the underpinning skills to support how you prepare for and use critical scrutiny within your placement agency and into your ASYE. This is not simply how you use supervision but how you develop dispositions towards professionalism within the team and in multi-professional working. Elsewhere I have explored the nature of the 'virtuous social worker'. That is, one whose practice is exemplary even when they are not under scrutiny, for to do otherwise would make them worried, feel sick or be unable to sleep. I know that many students have these attributes on entering the course but others work hard to develop them. This chapter will open up the skills you will need to become a virtuous social worker, encapsulating the nature of critique, rather than criticism; honesty and transparency replacing secrecy or subterfuge; bravery versus the 'it will be alright' mentality and recognising and celebrating your successes even where intervention does not go as planned. The aptitudes you develop in supervision will equip you to deal professionally with the shifting and contested nature that is contemporary social work.

By the end of this chapter you will be able to:

- analyse and critique the organisational aspects and documentation of the supervisory and tutor relationships;

- use supervision to prepare for and manage the complexities of practice;

- critically evaluate and engage in deep-level thinking about practice through supervision, including setting oneself follow-up activities to enable the development of critical dialogue with the practice educator and, where appropriate, off-site supervisor;

- identify, and act upon areas of risk, rights and power relevant to your practice;

- receive and act positively upon feedback from practice and assessments on practice.

What is student supervision in social work?

The supervision of students in social work has a distinct meaning because it is integral to professional values and beliefs. It considers experience, the inherent habitus of both the supervisee and the practice educator (supervisor), the agency remit, practice and protocol. Along with the educational requirements of nurture within adult learning these attributes form the core of your beginning ASYE and beyond. Within the placement, social work students are subject to a developmental trajectory that places them on a journey of reflective, reflexive and critical learning. Whatever their abilities at entry, students must eventually achieve competence through evidencing the key roles, elements and units, and the HCPC code of ethics for social work students. It is the process of supervision that will support you through this process. Such supervision bears no resemblance to the work supervision that micromanages and tolerates no mistakes, where control and instruction are held and given by the supervisor.

Here are a few definitions of the purpose of social work supervision.

> *Supervision enables students to practise their emerging social work self as well as reflect on this self. Thus supervision is an important place to consider the constitution of the professional self.*

(Dunk-West, 2013, p123)

Supportive elements of supervision occur in organisations that are:

> *responsible, productive and creative and where errors are seen as vehicles for learning.*

> (Argyris and Schon in Adams et al., 2009a, p381)

Edmondson structures student social work supervision into four sections:

- *Management and administration – a reporting phase checking that organisational standards and expectations, accountability, ethics and action plans are met.*

- *Learning and professional development – opportunities for reflection, celebration and challenge, explore dilemmas and offer opportunities for training and development.*

- *Exploration and discovery – identifying hidden talents or lacking skills, attributes and attitudes that should be applauded, changed or developed and opening up new areas for exploration.*

- *Support – opportunities for honest appraisal, critical self-reflection, the impetus to carry on and to bear the emotional content of the work within a non-judgemental environment.*

> (Edmondson, 2014, p140)

A deeper 'critical' level to supervision is proposed by Phillipson as:

> *Regrowing supervision for critical social work . . . in an era of challenge and contestation . . . where the work would be problematised. Emancipatory practice might well take place in the everyday activities of social work practices as well as the more usually assumed wider political spheres or indeed in both. What might it be like to have 'emancipatory practice' as an addenda item?*

> (Phillipson, 2009, pp188–94)

Howe proposes a central place for the exercise and development of 'emotional intelligence' within social work supervision:

> *Support and supervision for social workers help create a space for 'emotional thinking'. Supervision has many elements including containment, case management, information sharing and professional education. However, in its traditional form, supervision contains significant elements of self-reflection and analysis in which social workers think about how clients are affecting them emotionally and how they emotionally affect clients.*

> (Howe, 2008, p186)

Who will supervise me?

Student social workers have reported that the type of supervision they receive differs greatly depending on their supervisor and the agency within which they are placed. Preparing for supervision is, therefore, of immense importance to you as you will take responsibility for your own learning. An understanding of what the texts have shown you about the development of your professional self will enable you to go forearmed with your own agenda of how you learn, what you would like to accomplish and your expectations of your practice educator. Your practice educator will be both a qualified social worker and practice educator (or working towards this status in the case of the latter). In some cases your practice educator may be off-site with a work supervisor taking responsibility for the allocation of work on-site. Each will be involved in your supervision, as follows:

1. On-site practice educator

   This will be a qualified social worker and practice educator responsible for profes-sional supervision and the allocation of your work. They will enter into debates to encourage your critical thinking, use of theory to practise and vice versa, enable links to promote inter-team, inter-agency and multi-disciplinary/professional working, ver-ify and sign off your evidence to support the key roles and HCPC code of ethics for students, complete a report to be included in your portfolio to be presented to the assessment board, deal with any issues of sickness, misconduct, anti-discriminatory/ oppressive practice, prepare reports and attend meetings where required. It is their duty to raise awareness of any difficulties with a student's practice that arises on the placement. They will have two to three meetings, to include the tutor. They will com-plete two to three direct observations of the student's practice.

2. Off-site practice educator

   As above but with the exception of the allocation of work and the links to teams and other agencies. Supervision will normally be through discussion with the student and occasional three-way meetings to include the on-site job supervisor and two to three meetings also with the tutor that might also include the on-site supervisor. They will be responsible for the student report.

3. Job supervisor

   The student and job supervisor are likely to work together on a daily basis on-site. Any management issues, working relationships, agency policy, culture, protocols, application of the law, formal guidance, risk management, health and safety and disciplinary matters will be within their province. They will attend approximately three three-way meetings with the off-site practice educator and student and may participate in the meetings with tutors. They will contribute to the student report and might comment on placement-based student assignments. They may also undertake to complete one of the direct observations of the student's practice.

ACTIVITY 4.1

Define the most appropriate person to support you in each of the following situations.

1. *You have a dental appointment and need to ask for time off from the placement.*

2. *You are unsure what theory the placement prefers its workers to use.*

Continued

3. Your car has broken down and you are unable to complete an important visit.

4. You have a problem at home and are unable to complete a piece of assessed placement-linked work on time.

5. You have a difficult relationship with one of your work colleagues in placement.

6. You are concerned about doing a risk assessment and presenting this to a large case conference.

7. Your tutors keep talking about 'social constructions' but you cannot seem to get your head round how to apply it in the placement.

8. You overheard an administrative worker saying that one of the other workers only got the job because he is black.

9. Your on-site job supervisor is very busy and you have not had time to discuss any of your cases with him. Another member of staff is allocating your cases to you.

10. The agency does not have a social worker on the staff and you are finding it difficult to know what your role is.

COMMENT

Some solutions are clear cut. Anything to do with accountability to your daily routine in placement should be addressed to the on-site supervisor/practice educator (1, 3). Those issues to do with reflection, theory and assessed work should be addressed to the practice educator either on- or off-site (2, 4, 7). However, some areas are less clear and really involve both the on-/off-site practice educator and the job supervisor. In these cases (5, 6, 8, 9, 10) the practice educator will usually work through some of the possible solutions with you in supervision. They will suggest strategies and ask you to work through some of these too in order to develop ways that you might deal with these situations. It will not be their role to step in and solve these situations for you but to encourage you to seek and apply solutions yourself. In the event that the practice educator is posing the problem, the initial learning agreement should have identified another person who could be approached.

Why is supervision in social work so important?

This summary is taken from the Care Council for Wales pamphlet entitled 'Supervising and Appraising Well: A Guide to Effective Supervision and Appraisal for those working in Social Care'.

> *Effective performance management and improvement is one of the most important elements in ensuring positive outcomes for service users and carers who use social care services. It also has a crucial role to play in the development, retention and motivation of the social care workforce.*

What are the benefits of supervision and appraisal?

For the organisation:

- *Supporting the social care worker to understand the organisational values, also what outcomes the organisation is working to and how they contribute to these.*

- *Ensuring that service users and their carers receive a quality service.*

- *Enabling understanding and implementation of policies and procedures.*

- *Improving internal communication.*

- *Sharing responsibility for achieving outcomes.*

- *Promoting staff retention.*

- *Reducing rates of grievances, sickness and complaints.*

- *Supporting the social care worker to achieve the organisation's outcomes and standards.*

- *Promoting clear communication between the organisation and the social care worker.*

- *Ensuring that the social care worker has a manageable and appropriate workload.*

- *To adhere to the relevant Care and Social Services Inspectorate Wales (CSSIW) National Minimum Standards and the Care Council for Wales' Code of Practice for Social Care Workers.*

- *Promoting good practice.*

For the professional social care worker:

- *Supports the social care worker to be clear about his or her responsibilities and accountabilities and competent in his or her role.*

- *The opportunity to reflect on, analyse and evaluate practice.*

- *Enables setting, agreeing and reviewing SMART (specific, measurable, achievable, realistic, timely) goals and objectives.*

- *Provides constructive feedback.*

- *Promotes consistency of practice.*

- *Recognises and values good practice.*

- *Supports the health and well-being of the social care worker.*

- *Supports people to understand their role in the social care workforce.*

- *Reinforces clear professional boundaries.*

- *Promotes self-confidence.*

- *Identifies learning and development needs.*

- *Identifies possible coaching and mentoring needs.*

- *Develops team working.*

- *Increases transparency and openness.*

For the service user:

- *A worker is clear about their roles and duties and has had opportunities to discuss and develop their learning, enabling the provision of quality care services.*

- *A worker who has a clear understanding of the requirements of the Code of Practice for Social Care Workers.*

(Care Council for Wales, 2012, pp6–7)

The benefit for social workers is clearly stated in the document and the following research summary also shows that effective supervision can lead to enhanced support for staff and ultimately retention through reflective practice, job satisfaction, better critical abilities, emotional support, the perceived expert support from supervisors, empowerment and positive feedback.

RESEARCH SUMMARY

The SCIE published a research briefing (43) into effective supervision in social work and social care.

Key messages (author's emphasis):

- *Research has demonstrated that good supervision is associated with **job satisfaction, commitment to the organisation and retention.***

- *Supervision appears to **help reduce staff turnover** and is significantly linked to employees' **perceptions of the support** they receive from the organisation.*

- *Good supervision is correlated with perceived **worker effectiveness**. There is some evidence that group supervision can **increase critical thinking**.*

- *Supervision works best when it pays **attention to task assistance, social and emotional support** and that workers have a **positive relationship with supervisors**.*

- *The emotionally charged nature of the work can place particular demands on people in the field. It is important to provide **opportunities for reflective supervision**.*

- *In an inter-professional context, workers relate job satisfaction and professional development to their **supervisor's expert knowledge**, regardless of whether respondents shared the same professional background.*

- *The impact of supervision on outcomes for service users and carers has rarely been investigated. Anecdotal evidence suggests that **supervision may promote empowerment, fewer complaints and more positive feedback**. Overall, the empirical basis for supervision in social work and social care in the UK is weak. Most of the evidence is correlational and derives from child welfare services in the US.*

*The following link will take you to the SCIE report on effective supervision in social work and social care: **www.scie.org.uk/publications/briefings/files/briefing43.pdf***

Preparing for supervision

Taking from the above Care Council's documentation for social care workers, it is possible to extract the areas on which you should be focusing in order to gain the greatest benefit from your practice educator and interweave these with the PCF and HCPC requirements.

ACTIVITY **4.2**

Here are some of the descriptors for the need for supervision taken from the Care Council for Wales. Choose one from each section and imagine you are preparing for your next supervision session. I have tried to group them according to a timeline through the placement. Write one prompt note that you might include in a reflective log for each of these timelines.

First sessions:

- *be clear about your responsibilities and accountabilities and competent in your role*

- *set, agree and review your SMART (specific, measurable, achievable, realistic, timely) goals and objectives*

After work allocation and ongoing:

- *reflect on, analyse and evaluate practice*

- *accept and plan for constructive feedback*

- *be consistent in your practice*

- *be clear about professional boundaries*

- *develop self-confidence*

- *identify your learning and development needs*

- *recognise and value good practice*

- *acknowledge the need to monitor your health and well-being and deal with emotional stress*

- *appropriately seek help*

- *develop team working skills and practice*

Final placement phase:

- *identify possible coaching and mentoring needs*

- *work in ways that are transparent and open*

> COMMENT
>
> *Using the SMART goals (specific, measurable, achievable, realistic, timely) or SWOT framework (strengths, weaknesses, opportunities, threats; see also page 59) documents is one way you can begin to prepare for supervision. Your practice educator may also have a learning styles questionnaire that they have successfully used in the past, for example, that of Honey and Mumford which looks at various characteristics of learning styles – activists, reflectors, theorists and pragmatists. You can find this exercise at **www. brianmac.co.uk/documents/hmlsq.pdf**; complete it to find out what sort of a learning style you have.*

Reading the agency documentation will give you ideas about what is expected of you. For example, the mission statement, policies on risk, health and safety and lone working policies will guide your practice.

The frequency and length of supervision sessions should be discussed in your first supervision session. These often begin on a weekly basis, move to fortnightly in the middle section of the placement and then revert to weekly when the portfolio evidence is being worked on. Think about how to ensure that these are booked into diaries and what to do if they get postponed.

For ongoing work, decide what sort of agenda you would work to in supervision; for example, where a meeting starts at 1.00 pm:

1.00–1.30 Practical discussion of work carried out. Any information needed, cases to be closed or need for ongoing discussion.

1.30–2.00 Dilemmas and tensions in the work and reflection (you should summarise your reflective log here).

2.00–2.45 Critical analysis of the impact of your work. What went well and why, links to key roles and HCPC, alternative ways of working.

2.45–3.00 Allocation of new work/clarification of follow-up work and identification of any training, mentoring, information needs.

Think about how you would like to receive a critique of your work. You are a student and so it is not expected that you will know everything; few qualified workers would adhere to this claim, so you can expect to get things wrong. Most students want to know if they have done something wrong but they also emphasise being told when they have practised well. Check out when it is acceptable to use other team members as a resource, providing they are not busy and ensure you know the professional boundaries in speaking to more senior or experienced staff. These might seem like obvious points but it is important for you to remember that the practice educator and team have taken on a student as an additional responsibility within their already pressured workload. Set yourself follow-on activities to enable the development of critical dialogue. Try to use your emotional intelligence and sense when assessing whether it is okay to ask for information or help and when it is not.

Remember to take care of your own emotional state and, if stressed, take this to supervision. The practice educator will be able to give you coping strategies that will help you in your subsequent working life.

In the lead up to your final supervision sessions you will be presenting evidence of your ability to meet the key roles and HCPC guidance, and reviewing, closing and handing over your caseload. In this final phase, think about any unmet learning needs you have and how you might seek out appropriate people to help you to develop.

Although it is important that you develop openness and transparency throughout the placement it is during the collection of evidence that you will have opportunities to question your own motivations, values and prejudices. We all have areas of work that we find difficult because of our own beliefs and it is worth using these final sessions to open up some debate about how we can manage to practise ethically through recognising their presence and how to deal with them. Some students have said they could not work with criminals, troubled teenagers, people who are mentally ill for example, yet when these ideas are opened up in the placement they have often realised that their prejudice stems from ignorance and a fear of the unknown. In the final placement phase you will hopefully have developed a good working relationship with your practice educator and so it is a good time to let your imagination and creativity flow. Employ some magical thinking in debating and rethinking practice.

Analysing and critiquing documents used for supervision

Here are some of the documents that you may be working with in supervision within the practice agency and with your practice educator:

- learning styles questionnaire;
- agendas used in supervision;
- minutes and note taking;
- direct observation pro forma;
- key role framework;
- HCPC framework;
- reflective log;
- critical incident log;
- theory matrix;
- case studies;
- role-play scripts;
- agency recording and conferencing;
- case recordings (mostly online);

- university placement pro formas – requests, pre- and mid-placement forms;
- concerns meeting minutes;
- suspension from placement record;
- health and safety procedures;
- agency counselling request;
- reflection on good/poor practice accounts.

Apologies if this seems like a long list – and it is not exhaustive – but you can be certain that every professional tool will be used to ensure that you are safe to practise and have attained the required levels within the professional body – the HCPC, the key roles and the Quality Assurance Agency (QAA) social work benchmarks.

Some of this documentation will be designed to conform to the agency requirements – the **administrative/managerial accountability**. It is crucial that you are able to demonstrate to your practice educator that you are aware of their significance to the legal authority of the agency – their remit – and that in a court of law your documentation will be timely, accurate and fit for purpose. You might, however, feel able to offer a critique of these documents in supervision, particularly with regard to the nature of anti-oppressive practice.

ACTIVITY **4.3**

Have a look at one piece of your agency documentation and give a personal critique. For example, you might use an assessment form, a policy statement or procedural guidance. Try to look beyond the words and critically examine the impact it would have on staff and service users.

Look at this case study of how Sonia dealt with some misgivings she had about a risk assessment form.

CASE STUDY **4.1**

Sonia was disturbed by the wording of the risk assessment documentation in her placement that seemed to have a wholly negative focus. It seemed to ask questions that were negatively posed and seated the disadvantage with the individual instead of with their interaction with society. Poor families were asked about their children's sleeping arrangements and toys, the number of hot meals they had and what external activities/hobbies they took part in. Sonia felt that these questions further oppressed families who were living in states of dire poverty. She proposed that the questions be reviewed to reflect both the family's strengths in combatting such disadvantage (e.g. using other objects

Continued

CASE STUDY 4.1 *continued*

to replace toys, being creative in accessing free activities) and in centrally recording the unmet needs of such families within the agency's operational area. This way of working created a duality for Sonia in that she wanted to change the system but had to continue to work towards the agency remit. However, she felt more empowered through discussing this in supervision and working with her practice educator in finding a way to present her ideas to management.

Other aspects of the documentation will be solely used between you and your practice educator and lead towards the framing of evidence for your portfolio. These will be linked to the **educational/instructive purpose** of supervision. If you have a particularly suitable way of learning that you find helpful then you will need to explore this with your practice educator at an early meeting. They might have their own model and it would be useful for you to try that too. It can be risky to let go of what we know and what seems to work for us but an opportunity to try another way is often fruitful.

ACTIVITY 4.4

Think about some ways of learning that you have never tried. Maybe you feel too exposed by a discursive debate where you have to defend your ideas, or in demonstrating your learning by giving a presentation. Perhaps you feel that the practice educator's learning styles matrix is just a gimmick and it has not helped you.

Write a commentary for your learning log to say just how you would like the learning documentation to build on your ability to learn.

COMMENT

You might initially feel that you want to stay with tried and tested learning tools. Maybe, like many adults, you find that 'learning by doing' is the best way for you. You might prefer your practice educator to recommend some reading, websites or a significant person for you to interview or visit alongside. (Tried and Tested = TT)

There might be some tools with which you are unfamiliar, such as how to structure an agenda, take minutes of supervision sessions or write a critical incident report. You will also be working with tangible documents such as the key roles and HCPC framework and with formal agency documentation. How you evidence your practice will deepen through the placements so that although you are familiar with the format, your examples and critical writing will develop a deeper and more critical style. Case recordings will follow a clear format and are usually completed online, but the system and format in which they are stored might be different in each placement. (New and Set = NS)

Continued

COMMENT *continued*

Some learning styles can be highly creative, innovative and allow you to think outside the box of everyday practice. Constructing a role-play, writing a critical incident log or offering alternatives to received knowledge and practice also fall into this category. For example, you might work through using alternative theories with your practice teacher, create a team learning resource, offer to chair a team meeting, explore the impact of government policy or anti-discriminatory and anti-oppressive practice on service users. These are likely to be new learning activities that you will use as evidence towards your key roles and the HCPC code of ethics. (Critical and Creative Learning = CCL)

If it is useful, you can think about this formula that indicates the deeper levels of learning as expressed in documentary evidence you will use for your portfolio.

$$TT \longrightarrow NS \longrightarrow CCL$$

Case Study 4.2 looks at Ben, a student who had the courage to try something different to his usual 'safe' style of learning.

CASE STUDY 4.2

Ben knew that he learnt best through reading up on things. His practice educator raised some issues about his practice that he felt uncomfortable with. Some of the staff said Ben seemed aloof and he did not mix with them or seem to want to talk with them. One of the service user feedback comments on his first observation had said that Ben did not seem to be interested in her problems. A community psychiatric nurse in the multi-disciplinary team had found Ben to be arrogant and rude when she had spoken to him on the phone.

Ben asked his supervisor if she could recommend some policy documents and books to help him to improve. She said although she could do this it might not be the best way to help him. She suggested that they write some scripts and do some role-play exercises, possibly video them, and then discuss strategies for development together using a set of questions that they develop together to form his learning framework.

Although Ben found the idea of this daunting he agreed to it. The sessions turned out to be great fun, with the practice educator playing devil's advocate and often swapping roles with Ben. He subsequently began to do the role playing in his head before going on a visit, used his emotional intelligence with staff and attempted to use an inclusive approach when working with other professionals that saw him jointly focusing on the service user needs. Ben's learning needs in this case would not have been so expertly dealt with by reading texts.

Some documentation relates directly to the **supportive/evaluative purpose** of supervision. This might include working with the key roles, HCPC framework, reflective and

critical incident logs, theory matrices and observation pro formas. It is always pref-
erable for students to record their evidence contemporaneously. If you get a better
example you can always swap it later. Invariably, practice educators can see elements
of your practice that you fail to identify. In the main these are positive factors that
you cannot see about yourself. You might remember the part of the Johari window
where there are things you do not know about yourself but others do! In a direct
observation a practice educator will pick up things that you are unaware of and that
you are doing well. These might be to do with your personality such as good listening
skills, or to do with your knowledge, for example, knowing the law, policy and procedures correctly. Students generally underestimate their own abilities so the practice
educator has a role in pulling out good practice but also in evaluating effectiveness,
confidence, maturity and reasoned and appropriate behaviour. Therefore, support is
tempered with evaluation in establishing the development of an independent and
autonomous professional.

ACTIVITY 4.5

*Using your critical skills, be honest and think about what you know you do well and what
you might need help with. It might be useful to develop a self-questioning framework or
use the one given in Table 4.1. Look at the 'attributes' and underline the areas you might
need help with. Then compile a list of activities that would enable you to achieve them.*

Table 4.1   Stages towards asking critical questions

Question type	Description	Attributes
Fundamental	What do I think/know about X?	Describing, underpinning points with quotations.
Connecting	How does X relate to Y and Z?	Judging, balancing different perspectives, identifying a major contender in the debate.
Hypothesis	If X relates to Y and Z then A.	Consolidation, creativity, positioning a new perspective.
Critical	How can I defend my argument in evaluating X, Y, Z and A?	Contemplation, lateral thinking, conceptualisation of micro and macro debates and posing insightful explanations, solutions and/or challenges.

Source: Jones (2013, p9)

COMMENT

*Most students very quickly develop skills in the 'fundamental' area. As your first year
progresses you become more advance in how to juxtapose the areas of an argument
that 'connect'. You can see the positive and negative aspects of an argument. The next
two stages are often more complex for students because they involve your use of self
in the creation of new understandings. In the 'hypothesis' stage you will be using new
knowledge, letting go of old positions and reframing learning to come to a new position. Sometimes this is referred to as 'synthesis' – the ability to appreciate new positions*

Continued

COMMENT *continued*

from the acquisition of new knowledge. It involves a deep engagement with the subject or theme and asks the question: 'So what, now I know all that, how does it impact on me, the service user and the agency?' The 'critical' phase involves your creativity, EI and AI, your willingness to put your head above the parapet of received practice and wisdom, and to expand the application of your learning out to a global interpretation. These last two phases are the ones that students tend to focus on in their placements in supervision with their practice educators.

Have a look at Case Study 4.3 concerning Bav, who was a good student but made a serious error of judgement in her placement. Had she taken her ideas into this reflective tool she would have realised the importance of taking a step back from her emotions and recording strategies for cooling her passions. Recognising that there are more appropriate ways of dealing with the things that we feel strongly about is a sign of professional maturity.

CASE STUDY **4.3**

Bav was quite a young student but had a lot of life experience as she was a live-in carer for her ailing grandmother. Initially, her practice educator was impressed with her maturity and gave her quite a lot of access to senior management discussions. At a large meeting with the agency chief executive Bav inappropriately took a private telephone call and when asked by the CEO to please switch off the phone declined to do so stating that 'this is an example of how power is used to discriminate against the powerless' (she equated her position as a student with the latter). The issue was escalated throughout the agency and the practice educator was called to account for his student's behaviour. He could see that Bav was applying what she had been learning at university about power and oppression – though somewhat mistakenly.

He interpreted this as indicating a need for reflection from his student and was keen to use it as a learning experience for her. In their next supervision session the fallout from her behaviour was discussed with Bav and she was asked to complete a pro forma of a reflective account to be used in supervision, sent to her tutor and given to the CEO. This she did and fully realised that she had behaved inappropriately. Her practice educator said: 'You are like a young colt trying to charge at the world with your new knowledge. Now you see that there may be other, calmer and more professional ways to change things.' The completed pro forma on 'reflection' was used in her portfolio as evidence of her ability to reflect and change. This was a good learning experience for Bav and reminiscent of the previous quote from Argyris and Schon at the top of page 78.

Finally, where difficult decisions have to be made regarding a student's practice then the practice educator's role could become one of **discerning/scrutinising** with a view to making a fail recommendation. There are no formulaic documents for this other than the record of evidence itself and referencing the HCPC code of ethics. However, it is usual for a process of 'informal concerns' followed by 'formal concerns' meetings to present reports to the University Practice Panel for their decision as to whether the student should have a further placement opportunity or fail. The practice educator, student and tutor will present reports, and a representative of the practice placement team who chaired the formal concerns meeting might also be asked to present a report. Often, where students are not succeeding in the placement there are feelings of being unsupported, a lack of adequate supervision and feeling all at sea. If these are not brought to supervision there is a danger that students become stateless between being afraid to ask questions, taking action that is inappropriate or giving incorrect information to service users. This resultant unprofessional practice then becomes the root of scrutiny and, in some students' eyes, victimisation. The whole situation then becomes more than its constituent parts.

ACTIVITY *4.6*

What might you think and feel if your practice educator says s/he wants to have an informal concerns meeting to include your tutor?

Write down how you would set about preparing for this meeting.

COMMENT

Your first thoughts would probably be towards the evidence base for your practice framed around the documentation you had been using in supervision. Had you presented enough evidence of the right calibre? If tasks had been agreed with you, had these been achieved, if not the first time, then through being given a further opportunity? Had you followed agency policy and procedure correctly and completed and logged confidential documents correctly? Had the supervision sessions felt accommodating or challenging? There is nothing wrong with challenging so long as it is not threatening or demeaning of your practice. Did you feel all at sea, and if so how had you attempted to ground yourself?

Have a look at Paul's dilemma in Case Study 4.4.

CASE STUDY *4.4*

Paul had enjoyed his support work with older service users with a voluntary agency before deciding to train as a social worker. On placement he had received some poor feedback from the social work staff. He had fallen asleep during an interview with a service user (a senior social worker had allowed him to shadow her home visits). His practice educator had asked him to research the requirements of legislation for this service user group via the internet. He had spent two full days doing this but could not relate his findings to his practice educator in supervision. The team found him uncommunicative, with poor body

Continued

language and could hardly tell what he said as he mumbled. Two cases had to be removed from the student as he did not know how to plan for an interview. He had been very upset and emotional about telling an older couple, where the wife had dementia, that they could not be accommodated together. Developments agreed in supervision did not happen and the student eventually went off sick. An informal concerns meeting was held and a collaborative agreement made with Paul as to what targets had to be met within the next two weeks.

Subsequently, at the formal concerns meeting targets had not been met and the student used the opportunity to present his report as a vehicle to accuse the practice educator of failing to give proper supervision. All formal procedures had been followed and documentation produced but the student felt dissatisfied.

At a subsequent meeting (the student continued with the academic degree but without the social work qualification) the student said he had not realised the true nature of social work and it was not what he wanted. He appeared happy and spoke clearly and confidently, saying that he had felt depressed by the work and had been given anti-depressant medication by his doctor. In this case, the practice educator had used supervision and formal reports to nurture the student through testing abilities that Paul was unable to meet. He had used his agendas and minutes from the meetings, feedback from staff and service users and supervision notes documenting where tasks were not completed satisfactorily. The practice educator, seeing his role as nurturing, had to become the scrutiniser in order to uphold the professional conduct and ethics of social work.

Managing the complexity of supervision

Critical evaluation and deep-level thinking are needed if you are to grasp, understand and develop practice that can manage the complexity of contemporary social work. Some tools to prepare for and use in supervision that will help you to develop this level of thinking about your practice are:

- reflective journals;
- narrative accounts;
- critical incident analysis;
- learning journals;
- daily learning logs;
- presentations to staff/focus groups.

Activities that expose critical blockers and drivers for your learning and practice are derived from the following:

- opportunities to stand back from practice;

- outward facing perspectives that look beyond the organisation and staff group;

- problematisation of the status quo;

- challenge ideas such as 'it has always been this way' while celebrating successful continuity;

- search for meaning in actions;

- examine the impact of your own values and beliefs on your practice;

- pose moral and ethical dilemmas.

Your use of self in these activities will involve the development of your praxis, emotional intelligence and bravery – to challenge received truths, empathy, synthesis towards new positions based on knowledge, skills and experience. The strengthening of your confidence will result from the ongoing search to deepen your abilities, apply new learning and to move out of your comfort zone in taking risks to develop your practice. You should never feel you can tick off such development from your list. This persona should move with you throughout your career and one's motto should always be to know more tomorrow than you know today. It is this inherent aptitude that will give you the edge in seeking employment and in moving through your professional development.

A useful focus for complexity within supervision is to look at the nuances around risk assessment. Beck writes about the fact that social workers are constantly required to search for ways to identify and manage risk effectively. This is because the society in which we live has moved from risk being seen as an act of God, due to human fecklessness or just bad luck, to being the result of human action or failure to act. The idea of identifying, assessing and managing risk is now a core activity, not only of social workers but also of actuaries, financial institutions, health professionals, police and emergency services and insurance companies.

The social model assessment of risk commonly used in social work tends to focus on a strengths approach. This means that although potential dangers are recognised they are balanced against the compensating factors of systemic positives. For example, an assessment of a family situation indicating that a child might be at risk can be ameliorated to some extent by the presence of a supportive local network – friends, family and local nursery and good relationships with a midwife/health visitor. An assessment of a family which raises slight worries about a child may ring alarm bells if the family is isolated and unwilling to cooperate with the professionals as listed above.

ACTIVITY **4.7**

Focusing on the concept of risk and within a supervision session, develop a set of critical questions that you want to discuss with your practice educator that you draw from the following narrative.

CASE STUDY 4.5

Saffi is an asylum seeker awaiting leave to remain in the UK. She is currently given financial support from the UK Border Agency. Saffi has a medical condition, requiring an operation, that means she will be dependent on the supply of medical provisions once she has received her leave to remain. You have been asked to support her through her operation and beyond.

Over the six weeks you have been working with Saffi she shares with you that her condition has been caused by sexual abuse by male members of her family over a period of 20 years. She was imprisoned by them and prevented from having any outside contacts. She was freed and brought to the UK by Amnesty International.

Your practice educator is sympathetic but believes that Amnesty International is responsible for working with Saffi as yours is a short-term referral team only. Also, your supervision session has been cancelled three times due to your practice educator being asked to take on some managerial duties for the agency.

Think through a clear picture of your grasp of the risk factors for Saffi prior to developing a robust defence for your continuing work with her to your practice educator. She is vulnerable, isolated in this country, and has undergone imprisonment and torture for many years. She is about to have a major operation after which there will be a considerable recovery time during which she will need support carers, home nursing and social care provision. If she obtains leave to remain her resourcing will cease from the UK Border Agency and she will need help to apply to other sources. If all goes well with her recovery she will need further surgery to enable her to lead a more normal life.

Following from this initial, descriptive account prepare to create your defence in the following theoretical way. First, you might think about how emancipatory values might influence your views of risk. Pease and Fook (1999) refer to how the theories of critical realism might influence emancipatory theory. Archer et al. (1998) see this as a developmental strategy to fuse the narratives of service users and social workers in the recognition of their differential knowledge, diversity and power. Anti-discriminatory and anti-oppressive practice are core themes in social work education and practice. As such, the constructive challenges to individuals, institutional and structural mechanisms in the areas of injustice, inequality and oppression are our moral purpose. It is surprising that such debates do not generally form the starting point of students' relationships with their practice teachers.

Second, there is much emotional engagement with Saffi's plight. Using self-reflection applied to reflexivity will enable you to seek out the critical questions to ask yourself about how to deal with this emotional content. Whether you agree with your practice educator's views or not you do need to recognise the agency policy, the availability of support elsewhere, the recent austerity cuts in your service.

However, this will be an opportunity to gather evidence for your portfolio through posing questions about the moral purpose of social work. You may question the move away from social work that was at the forefront of welfare reforms in the mid-twentieth century to the current implementation of 'government policies that restrict choice and ration resources . . . social work has not challenged detrimental policy changes' (Jordan, 2004, p6). Jordan further states that 'social work assists in the coercion of poor people into externally imposed self-improvement strategies, where they will fail in the competitive task of attaining excellence' (2004, p10). Jordan aligns himself with new collective movements utilising a community development approach as he sees the vulnerable as being unable to succeed, to exit their situation or to have a voice.

Third, following on from this Higham (2006, p139) states that 'the classic dilemma for social workers is that their advocacy for individuals is conducted from within organisations that often can oppress or restrict people's freedoms and opportunities'.

And finally, how might you link all this to how you feel about your practice educator cancelling your supervision sessions on three occasions? Does this serve to reinforce not only your service user's position but also your own as a student?

These four areas of criticality will underpin the functionalist areas of supervision because you will be linking them into the theories, strategies, methods, knowledge and skills used. Be sure that you apply the same rigour to these areas also. For example, critique the theory, policy and practices. Examine the social construction of the legislation, the managerial qualities of governance and the reality of practice as opposed to the requirements of procedure. Think about the assessment forms, meetings protocol, organisational hierarchy, disciplinary procedures, custom and practice, support mechanisms and team cohesion, along with the rights and risks for your service users. How might all of these influence your practice and what responses might you receive to challenges posed?

Universities have increasingly shifted the focus of assignments for social work students to include an emphasis on practice. This is partly due to the feedback from employers who want 'practice ready' employees. However, this does not mean there is no place for the interrogation of theory to practice and vice versa. Linking theory into the HCPC guidance on ethics and to your key roles will also give you opportunities for a more critical approach to your practice.

CHAPTER SUMMARY

Chapter 4 has given you some ideas about what type of supervision you can expect and by whom. You have hopefully understood why supervision is such an important part of your course and how to use the associated documentation to your advantage. Some strategies in how to prepare for your supervision sessions have been given. Finally, some of the complexity of managing the supervisory relationship was explored within the development of your ability to use criticality in your questioning, and through analyses that will support you as an NQSW and beyond.

Chapter 5 will progress this learning into the completion of the practice portfolio through the selection of substantial evidence-based practice examples, the use of effective signposting, an inclusion of theory to practice critical ideas stated with clarity, the marshalling of practice educator reports and evidence from significant professionals and service users.

FURTHER READING

Edmondson, D (2014) *Social Work Practice Learning: A Student Guide.* London: Sage.

Chapter 7, Introducing Risk in the Context of Social Work Practice Learning and Chapter 8, Using Supervision, Reflective Practice and Critical Thinking are key aspects of this book. The book uses numerous case examples including 'risk and the importance of social work supervision' on page 131. Models and types of supervision, preparation and barriers, use of contracts, reflection and critical thinking are juxtaposed with deep and surface approaches in Chapter 8. There is clear signposting to a comprehensive coverage of all practice-related themes, addressed directly to the student in an accessible style.

Keen, S, Gray, I, Parker, J, Galpin, G and Brown, K (2009) *Newly Qualified Social Workers: A Handbook for Practice.* London: Sage.

Although the title of the book indicates it is for NQSWs, Chapter 3 connects with the ideas of managing induction, probation and supervision that will not be unlike the levels currently being worked towards in this book. The performance criteria on pages 35–40 (Table 3.1) are particularly useful in implementing performance-related criteria.

USEFUL WEBSITES

www.scie.org.uk/publications/briefings/files/briefing43.pdf

Effective Supervision in Social Work and Social Care – a piece of research reported in 2012 demonstrating the positive outcomes to individuals and organisations on the value of effective supervision in social work and social care. You can get the main points by reading the executive summary at the beginning of the work.

YouTube: Supervision Role Play with sashas28us

www.youtube.com/watch?v=0K-OdXfS3Aw

This 38-minute clip covers broad aspects of an initial supervision session. It examines roles, responsibilities, methods and strategies. It also deals with ethnicity, theories, evidence requirements and supervisor's expectations. Strengths and weaknesses and learning objectives and goals are worked through with the student. The role-play gives a good balance of both supervisor and student 'voice'.

Chapter 5
Completing your portfolio

A C H I E V I N G   A   S O C I A L   W O R K   D E G R E E

This chapter will help you to develop the following capabilities, to the appropriate level, from the Professional Capabilities Framework:

- *Professionalism*: Describe the importance of professional behaviour; describe the importance of personal and professional boundaries.
- *Values and ethics*: Demonstrate awareness of own personal values and how these can impact on practice.
- *Diversity*: Recognise the importance of diversity in human identity and experience, and the application of anti-discriminatory and anti-oppressive principles in social work practice.
- *Rights, justice and economic well-being*: Understand the principles of rights, justice and economic well-being and their significance for social work practice.
- *Critical reflection and analysis*: Recognise and describe why evidence is important in social work practice.
- *Intervention and skills*: Demonstrate basic ability to produce written documents relevant for practice.

It will also introduce you to the following standards as set out in the 2008 Social Work Subject Benchmark Statement:

4.6   Critically reflect upon ethical principles and dilemmas.
5.1.2 The service delivery context.
5.1.3 Values and ethics.
5.1.5 The nature of social work practice.
5.5.4 Intervention and evaluation.
5.9   ICT and numeracy skills.
6.2   The learning process in social work.
7.3   Knowledge and understanding.

Introduction

Your placement learning so far has guided you from the personal preparation you need to make before going on placement (Chapter 1), and in the early days of settling in, to an appreciation of the structures and practices of your agency (Chapter 2). Chapter 3 gave you some ideas about how to drill down your learning to deeper and more critical levels, while Chapter 4 encapsulated your position within a supervisory relationship. Now, in Chapter 5 the discussion is around the gathering of evidence for your portfolio and the synthesis of theory and practice commensurate with an NQSW. Although descriptive elements are necessary, the main constituents of the portfolio should evidence your ability to critically think, question, reflect upon and evidence your abilities using the law, theory, knowledge, skills, methods, aptitudes, dispositions, procedures and intelligences. This guidance exemplifies for you how to write about the key roles and code of ethics in ways that lift your work from the descriptive.

By the end of this chapter you will be able to:

- select appropriate elements of your practice with which to evidence the key roles and code of practice using a variety of methods;

- express your evidence of practice using reflective and deep learning language skills;

- adhere to all aspects of confidentiality in consultation with agency staff, practice teacher and those who use the services of the agency;

- use skills of analysis and evaluation in synthesising theory and practice.

What is meant by 'evidence'?

The concept of evidence in general, and social work and research in particular, often relates to the application of scientific proof to actions, outcomes and consequences. The application of a theory, in a given situation, can be judged to be successful where the effect is commensurate with the predictive outcomes prescribed by the theory. For example, where behaviour should be ceased (non-school attendance) or promoted (developing child care skills), then cognitive behaviourism might be chosen. However, this sort of 'psychodynamic' approach is at odds with the more interpretive approaches that use collaborative and inclusive methods. The latter are developed through incremental processes of critical reflection alongside service users and with colleagues (Gould and Baldwin, 2004, p48). Examples of this might be where community social work, humanist approaches and reflective and evaluative methods are used.

Evidence-based practice (EBP) is currently seen to be integral to the development of a profession that can robustly defend its professionalism and reasons for action against the onslaught of the media when there are major failures to protect vulnerable children and adults (Forrester, 2011). Although presented here as the two binaries of scientific and reflective methods, these terms are too narrow to encapsulate the breadth and depth of what social workers do. Using theory, critical reflection, experience, intuition and inclusive approaches to evidence practice will be part of your collective pallet. While this offers an eclectic approach it is not a 'pick and mix' solution to the complexity of accountability through evidence of 'what works'. Your evidence must be presented in ways that demonstrate a highly competent melding of why and how you took action, what tools you deemed appropriate and why, how you dealt with dilemmas, what consequences resulted (or not) from your action, and finally that you adhered to the implementation of the law and policies and practices of your agency. In short, it is not sufficient to merely say that you did something.

What sort of evidence should be included in the portfolio?

In the previous paragraph the idea of there being several types of evidence appropriate to use in social work was mooted. There will be some that are 'functionalist' – to do with a technical rationalist approach to making accountability overt. For example, the completion of reports for deadlines, complying with agency policy and practice, collaborating in meetings and filling out forms.

Other types of evidence relate to a student's use of self-reflection, analysis and synthesis of their learning. The level of critical thinking they apply to this is reflected in the depth of the evidence, the language and ideas used to underpin their evidence and, ultimately, in the resilience used in undertaking the work. They can be seen to apply creative thinking through using a professional artistry approach and such students will often re-think their approach to practice even if all went well.

Bringing these two approaches together, research-minded students would use their practice evidence to inform a questioning and critical approach to their work. These are the first steps towards the creation of an EBP that recognises that research will never find absolute truths about practice, and have the integrity to work in collaborative and collective ways giving majority voice to those who use services. A useful term for this type of evidence is given by Pease (2007) where it is stated that:

> *I have suggested that critical realism seems to offer a reconciliatory position between positivism and social constructionism. I have thus proposed that critical social workers develop the foundation for 'critical knowledge-informed practice' to encompass critical social theory, quantitative and qualitative research, tacit knowledge, critical reflective practice, social justice values and consumer-based knowledge. Only a valuing of knowledge from diverse sources that is driven by a commitment to social transformation will enable social work to fulfil its emancipatory objectives.*

> (quoted in Adams et al., 2009b, p195)

On placement students can expect to be under scrutiny at all times so that all types of communication with colleagues, other agencies, service users, while on the phone and in electronic communications may be used as evidence of your practice, for good or bad. It is common practice for your practice educator to ask for feedback about your performance in these areas.

Sources of evidence

The evidence is framed around:

- The key roles (National Occupational Standards) numbered 1–6. Some programmes allocate key roles 1–3 to first placement and key roles 4–6 to final placement.

- The HCPC Guidance on Conduct and Ethics for Students – numbers 1, 2, 3, 6, 7, 8, 9, 10, 12, 13 (numbers 4, 5 and 11 apply to health professionals only).

To demonstrate your competence you will need to develop evidence through:

- taking on a small caseload appropriate to your student status and the agency;

- completing three direct observations of your practice (one must be before the mid-placement review, your practice educator must observe you at least twice, the observations must be undertaken in different activities, e.g. service user interview, meeting, while on duty);

- participating in supervision – showing a readiness to practise, compile an agenda and take minutes where required, keep your practice educator informed of your progress while offering critical appraisal of the work via your reflective log;

- engaging with your colleagues, team and other agencies in ways that represent your agency favourably;

- applying and critiquing theory, anti-discriminatory and anti-oppressive practice;

- identifying, analysing and managing risk and preparing evidential reports;

- keeping appropriate and timely records and compiling reports according to the agency practice;

- observing confidentiality yet being aware of where this is not possible due to risk;

- obtaining feedback from service users;

- keeping your own records of your learning journey for use in supervision and as evidence of your trajectory of development.

As you get to know the culture of the placement you might consider more creative evidence to include:

- analysis of role-play and simulations;

- application of reflective frameworks – e.g. Barnett;

- critical incident reviews;

- peer learning using the concept of critical friends;

- contributions to policy development in the agency;

- participation in training content and delivery;

- compilation of information files to signpost service users to the agency provision or to other agencies;

- forging partnership arrangements;

- conducting service user evaluations;

- undertaking complex cases.

Documents used for evidence might be:

- direct observation pro formas, including service user feedback;

- practice educator comments/notes/feedback, and records of supervision;

- written feedback from colleagues/other agencies;

- university–placement linked assignments;

- revelatory 'eureka' moments from your reflective log (hopefully you will have those);

- narrative accounts to promote learning, e.g. an account of how you have used frameworks for learning rather than giving descriptive accounts. (What did you learn, what impact did it have on you, how has it changed your understanding and practice, how did it relate to broader contexts, e.g. government policy, globalisation, social constructionism and discourse analysis?);

- proceedings from informal and formal concerns meetings;

- the placement mission statement, policy and practice guidance;

- health and safety guidance, for example, on procedures for lone working.

Hopefully these lists have given you plenty of ideas as to how you might gather your evidence. It is not exhaustive and you can be creative about what you consider 'evidence' so long as this is agreed with your practice educator. One of my tutees went on a 'development weekend' with a group of lone mums and their children who were service users. She had so much to put in her learning log that it was difficult to know what to use! She needed to commit her critical analysis to writing and use this in a supervision session though before it could be considered as evidence.

Preparing to compile the portfolio of evidence

Approaching your placements with a readiness to identify evidence of competence is essential. Although the portfolio is not presented for scrutiny until the end of the academic year you should begin to identify possible opportunities to include before you even begin the placement. Generally the placement agreement form, completed when you and your tutor initially visit the placement, will document your learning needs and the agency response to these. Figure 5.1 shows an example.

Figure 5.2 outlines some sources of portfolio evidence during the early stages of practice. This matrix can form the beginning of your evidence-base to be developed and critically examined with a view to providing substantial evidence for your portfolio. You should be keeping a reflective log and an ongoing record of the key role chart in which to deposit your evidence of competence. Have a look Activity 5.1 and try to expand on the type of evidence the stated practice opportunities might give you.

Learning needs	Practice opportunities
Legislation and policy	Completing a Team Around the Child report
	Using agency risk analysis pro formas
	Attending child protection court
	Undertaking agency training in use of MIS
Procedures	Introduction to culture of recording
	Eligibility criteria and time scales
	Office practice, accountability procedures, health and safety
	Undertaking duty social work rota
Theories to practice	Introduction to the usual theoretical positions used in the agency
	Extending theories learned in university to the placement
	Defending own position on your practice
	Sharing discussions in staff meetings
Models of multi-disciplinary work	Practice links to five agencies: CMHS, school, drug and alcohol unit, Police, Health Action Zone

Figure 5.1   *Agency response to meeting student learning need for evidence of competence in practice*

ACTIVITY **5.1**

Anticipating evidence

Create an example of evidence from each of the four areas shown in Figure 5.1.

How might you develop your evidence for inclusion in the portfolio?

COMMENT

Agency reports and pro formas are a usual way to gather evidence. However, think about how you researched what to use and how you linked it to the law under which your agency has a remit to practise. Did you ask if you could read colleagues' work that was of a high standard to inform your own work? Query how the policy has impacted on the agency practice and whether service users have any input into this.

When shadowing or attending court hearings you may have little opportunity for any interaction. However, you can prepare a narrative in your learning log after the event to draw out questions. Alternatively reposition yourself as the service user and think about what could have been done better from their perspective.

Students are generally welcomed onto any in-house training. Take all the opportunities to attend this and keep a record stating how useful it was and any areas for improvement.

Continued

If you found it useful then contact the training provider to thank them and say so. If you feel you have anything to offer, for example in the area of service user involvement, anti-discriminatory practice or some teaching from university then discuss this with your practice educator with a view to creating a small presentation or leaflet.

In the beginning of the placement you will be in the 'acclimatisation mode', getting used to the confusing array of procedures. Once you feel more comfortable with these and your practice educator, you might begin to critique them and make suggestions as to how they might be improved. For example, can you spot any duplication in the documentation or procedures, is the language inclusive and are there points in the system that block rather than drive the process forwards?

The use of theory in placement seems to pose difficulties for some students. It is often in their list of 'learning needs' and practice educators are asked to respond to how they will meet that need during the pre-placement meeting. The tutor might need to interpret the practical elements given by the practice educator during the meeting. This is because although theory is used, it seems to be so infused into practice that it is not articulated as pure theory itself. As a student you will need to demonstrate how you recognise, evaluate and use theory. This is because theory used in social work constitutes the bedrock of your practice. We will look at this again in Chapter 6. In practice you may take an eclectic approach, as human problems are rarely one-dimensional. If you are able to meld your approach to fit then it must be appropriate and not merely a snatching of odd methods. You might think about how each engagement with a service user has a journey. Rarely is the path straight, but normally will consist of a series of turn-offs, dead ends and circles. Each phase might need a different theoretical approach and you will become aware that some theories are compatible. For example, crisis intervention might lead to task-centred practice work, while a solution-focused approach could lead to or from a cognitive behavioural approach.

Think of colleagues from your own and other agencies as people who might contribute to evidence of your competence. Your practice educator will ask their opinions about you. This does not mean that you have to cultivate other practitioners by being popular and easy-going. You will need to be professional, using your emotional intelligence, advocacy skills and appropriately challenging poor practice. If you feel uneasy about challenge then work out with your practice educator how to improve in this area. Keep a critical incident log to help with this. Collaborative working is a highly valued tool alongside trustworthiness, honesty, integrity and resilience. Think about how you might make these skills visible and susceptible to inclusion in your portfolio.

Deepening the evidence

Key roles

I have written at length about the use of critical skills within the earlier chapters of this book, particularly with reference to Jan Fook, Daniel Goleman and Ron Barnett. I have also stated that your portfolio evidence must be more than writing

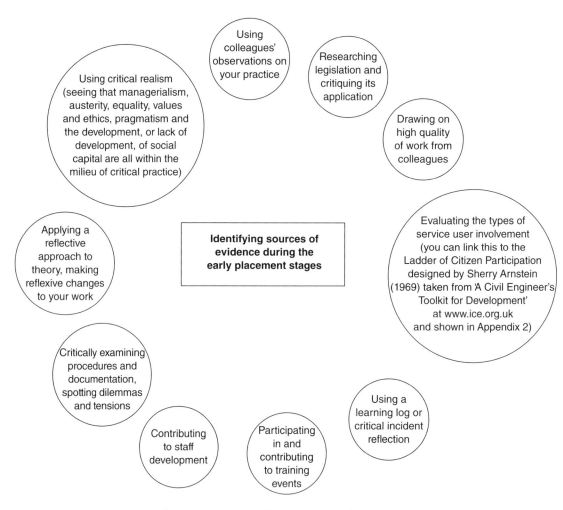

Figure 5.2 *Identifying sources of evidence of your practice during the beginning and early stages*

descriptively about what you did. Bringing these two themes together I have mentioned the notion of critical realism as 'critical knowledge informed practice' being the definition of Bob Pease.

This is the phrase you should have in mind as you select, reframe and swap evidence as you go through the placement. You should endeavour to journey through your evidence from the descriptive to the transformational in the following ways.

First, using **descriptive** narrative will give the context of your evidence. Second, you will be **reflecting** on your practice or the situation; standing back from the description and looking for meaning. Eventually, you might understand, through several reflective activities, what action is needed and, in working towards this, you become an agent of change. This change effectively alters your self-action for all future similar events and you become a **reflexive** practitioner, interested in praxis. The next phase will see your development move into **criticality**, for example, realising the lack of social capital that many service users have and the need for emancipatory under-standing and practice. This also means recognising the powerful position of social work and agencies that carry out social work. A further stage beyond criticality is the notion of **transformational** practice, involving a reconstruction of the self and a critique-in-action of the world. This might be how you have fashioned your new understandings around topics such as asylum seekers, female genital mutilation, the right to die. These are all complex debates seated in the social construction of 'others' and the discourses that both emanate from and feed into the lived experiences of the disadvantaged. This thinking, when it is informed by and informs your practice will give you plenty of deep evidence for the portfolio.

CASE STUDY **5.1**

Key role 4 – unit 12: Manage risk to individuals, families, carers, groups, self and colleagues.

*12.1 **Identify** and **assess** the nature of the risk.*

Evidence.

I worked with S, a 34-year-old lone mother with three children. There were concerns about the care of the children and S's own mental health as reported by the nursery, school and health visitor. Under the Children Act 2004 I was required to complete a TAC risk assessment using the agency report format that I presented to the Child Protection Safeguarding Panel. (Descriptive)

I reflected on S's vulnerability due to her mental health and her fears about the possibility of having her children removed. However, I was clear not to guarantee that this would not happen and that my role was to ensure the safety of the children. I was honest in saying that I would work with her to support her to improve the care of the children. I was con-cerned at the unkempt appearance of the children and the unhygienic state of the home. (Reflective)

S identified that she often failed to take her children to nursery and school because her anti-depressants made her oversleep. On one occasion the older child had attempted to make breakfast for the other children and had incurred a burn to her arm. The young-est child had an infected sore on his bottom due to wearing a nappy while at home. (Descriptive)

S was a warm and loving mother who the children seemed to have a good relationship with. The problems had arisen due to a lethargy caused by strong medication but this was rendering S incapable of safely caring for the children. S said she would like help with cleaning the home, washing and childcare. By negotiation she agreed to my contact-ing her GP with a view to seeking alternative medication with fewer side effects. These actions, once instigated, would give S a framework for recovery and involve professionals who could draw on strategies for change to support her. (Reflexive)

Continued

I was aware that S had no support from family or friends and lived in a slightly remote house on the edge of the town. She had moved to the area when she married and her husband had left just before the birth of the last child, and did not finance her in any way. In critically analysing her situation I realised she had reached a crisis after years of 'just managing'. As such she had tried numerous ways to cope and with each failure had sunk deeper into her depression. The situation was now serious yet her love of the children and vice versa was evident. However, the risks to the children were physical (unhygienic home, sores unchecked, danger of children using cooker), emotional (no socialisation with people outside the family, lack of education). Also the risks to S were her deteriorating mental health, the removal of her children, the unhygienic state of the house. S had few skills in self-advocacy due to repression in her own upbringing, she lacked confidence and was pessimistic about her and her children's futures. My assessment of S was that she was oppressed and I became aware that, although I wanted to try everything to support her, I may have to recommend action that would deny her the right to care for her own children. (Criticality)

Equality for such women is further denied through the action of the state through social workers, in referencing them against the norms of those who make policy. As a mother she was expected to be the prime carer yet when she failed was blamed and vilified by being seen as an unfit mother. Her script of helplessness, due to her mental ill health, reinforced public perceptions of her. I found dealing with my heart and head in this case very difficult, as I am also a lone mother. Regardless of this my focus remained on the care of the children. (Transformative)

The evidence throughout Case Study 5.1 includes descriptive, reflective, reflexive, critical and transformative statements and gives a deep flavour of the student's understanding of her practice. She has come to a new position on S and this knowledge will contribute to her beliefs and future practice.

The evidence in this case study also makes reference to the **management of risk** – by bringing in support services and the GP. This is mentioned in unit 13 of the same key role and so you might separate out this evidence. You may use the same case or service user to provide evidence covering a number of the units and elements of the key roles. Remember to scan back to the key role and unit for each piece of evidence for the element as it must demonstrate a coherence of the three statements of competence. There must be at least one piece of evidence for each of the elements and for each of the HCPC code of ethics for students.

Evidencing the HCPC code of ethics for students

Within this fictional account you can see that reference is also made to points within the HCPC guidance on conduct and ethics for students. For example:

2. Respecting confidentiality – by using S rather than the full name.

9. You should get informed consent – to contact the doctor.

12. You should behave honestly – not promising that the children would not be removed.

ACTIVITY 5.2

Strategies to deepen your portfolio evidence

Using the example of S and her children in the case example of key role 4.12.1, how might you separate out the complexities of the case and your thinking to demonstrate criticality?

REFLECTION POINT

Can you identify what the descriptive parts are and how they contribute to giving the context of the work? What knowledge would you draw on with which to reflect on how to make the assessment? How central would an attempt to create emancipatory practice be?

How much of your personal values and beliefs might influence the work? Would it make a difference to your reflection if S was from a minority ethnic background or she was disabled? Could she be considered a 'good enough parent', and on what might you base such an assessment? How much are you able to balance the enablement of S with the protection of her children, and what dilemmas might this pose for you? In what circumstances might you have to break confidentiality?

You will see that asking these critical questions places you in an anticipatory frame of mind. Increasingly you will not be entering initial visits with a blank frame of mind but with a repertoire of concerns to which you will be seeking answers. It is through a deepening of your knowledge and, consequently, evidential statements in your assessments and reflections in your learning log and in supervision, that you will garner the critical evidence for the portfolio.

Criticality, reflexive and reflective skills should be evidential in the mid-placement meeting. You will have opportunities to present your practice in a thoughtful and professional way. You might also be surprised to hear that your practice educator has observed your progression in ways that you have not realised. Hopefully these are positive contributions to the meeting. Where they are negative try to see these as opportunities for learning rather than confrontational. Tutors will ask your practice educator for a general overview of your practice and an indication as to whether you are working towards a pass. This is because the mid-point review must identify any areas of concern so that plans can be negotiated to offer supported opportunities to progress. Targets may be set at mid-placement to provide you with opportunities to demonstrate that you understand and are able to achieve the state of 'transformation' in your practice. You should be thinking about what this means for you and give your practice educator some indication of how you think you might achieve it.

You should not think that the key roles, elements and units, while being simply expressed, will be satisfied with simplistic responses.

Gathering evidence moving towards the end of placement

I have written earlier about being prepared to gather evidence from:

- the pre-placement meeting;

- familiarising yourself with the agency, policies, practice and staff;

- beginning to deepen your learning as you progress through the placement;

- the mid-placement meeting, where you will be consolidating and reflecting on your evidence so far.

Throughout this time you will need to be completing the key role document and the HCPC code of ethics. With your practice educator you should be identifying any gaps where you are having difficulty in finding evidence, and where you need to replace old evidence with better examples.

Now I want to focus on your critical themes and debates towards the end of placement and the identification of deep, rich evidence. Let us think about the purpose of social work. Here is a definition of social work by the International Federation of Social Work:

> The **social work** profession promotes **social** change, problem solving in human relationships and the empowerment and liberation of people to enhance well-being. Utilising theories of human behaviour and **social** systems, **social work** intervenes at the points where people interact with their environments.

> (IFSW, 2014)

The key points here are that social workers should:

- promote social change;

- solve problems of human relationships;

- use empowerment and liberation strategies;

- enhance well-being;

- use theories;

- work within social systems.

In 2002 the Topps UK partnership published a document indicating certain requirements of social workers. These were indicated by service users and their carers in tandem with the National Occupational Standards for Social Work, and were defined by Higham (2006) as 'clusters of expectations':

- *use of time;*

- *use of relationships and communication;*

- *use of assessment skills;*

- *service users' and carers' wishes for services that promote independence and recognise their own expertise;*

- *people who use services and carers want services that establish contact with a range of provision.*

(Topps, 2002, pp31–4)

The six key roles for social workers incorporate 21 supporting units of competence; see **www.hpc-uk.org**.

It is to all these statements that your final evidence will be addressed. In the first practice placement your evidence needs to demonstrate that you are 'competent' and in your final placement, that you are 'proficient'. Benner (2004), in her model of skills acquisition (using the Dreyfus (2004) model), defines these as:

'competent' – the competent practitioner no longer relies solely on rules and guidelines; uses maxims for guidance, according to the variable meaning of a situation, uses conscious deliberate planning and can perceive deviations from the normal pattern.

'proficient' – a proficient practitioner uses guidelines for action based on attributes or aspects, and after some prior experience can recognise the global characteristics of situations. The proficient practitioner now sees action at least partially in terms of longer-term goals, sees what is most important in a situation, and can cope with the crowdedness of pressurised contexts where there are many separate factors vying for attention.

Further, you should be positioning yourself as a virtuous social worker. McBeath and Webb have encapsulated the meaning of this (author's emphasis):

*The role of the virtuous social worker is shown to be one that necessitates appropriate application of intellectual and practical virtues such as **justice, reflection, perception, judgement, bravery, prudence, liberality and temperance**.*

This 'self-flourishing' worker, in bringing together the capacity for theoretical and practical action, makes possible a hermeneutic or interpretive praxis best appraised in dialogue with fellow-practitioners and clients.

(2002, pp1015–36)

Using virtue ethics in your portfolio evidence

Think about one area of your practice in placement and, taking one of the areas of virtue ethics, apply it to your practice. Then ask yourself one critical question. When you have answered this, ask yourself another.

Continued

For example:

- *bravery – making a decision not to admit someone into residential care.*

Why was this brave?

What could have been the consequences of my action?

How did/would I have defended my decision?

Who did I have to consider?

COMMENT

Our profession needs us to think not only about the work done but also about how it is done by social actors. What do you think social work is about? Is it about defensive decision-making, accountability, averse risk analysis and measurements of effectiveness? Or do you see it as being about emancipation, notions of the well-being of a defined community and the protection of the vulnerable? Perhaps it is all of these. In the example in Activity 5.3 would you have considered the views of family, friends and the media if your older service user had died as a result of falling downstairs? Despite the fact that you were respecting her wishes not to admit her, it would be seen that your failure to take appropriate action had resulted in her death.

What is it about how we do it? Unlike pure science where there is a formula and a 'right' solution, we are dealing with the uniqueness of individual states where we can never know what the 'right' answer is. In using the least intervention we aim to be prudent with resourcing but more than this is the argument of limiting the creation of dependency. We aim for a 'good enough' outcome but are unable to put the icing on the cake. We achieve the service level yet are aware of how much more could be done to increase service users' social capital, without which their progress is severely limited.

These tensions cause restlessness in the virtuous social worker that has to be satisfied. By networking, building strategic partnerships and using critical thinking skills, using theory and emotional intelligence you will build a resilience and be able to bear the stress and pressure that is symptomatic of contemporary social work practice. It is your demonstration of these ideas that will deepen the evidence for your portfolio – your ability to be self-flourishing in an unpredictable world.

Finally, consider how much social work is about 'control'. Are social workers merely agents of social control between those who have and those who have not? A buffer between chaos and regulation, between the malcontents and the upper classes? How do you assess your own use of power – is it legitimate or arbitrary?

Confidentiality and the portfolio evidence

There are two aspects to confidentiality and the portfolio. One relates to the principle of social work ethics and values and the protection of service user information; the other to the anonymisation of information given in the portfolio from which it may be possible to identify the service user(s) or carers.

Confidentiality in professional practice

- confidentiality is one of the casework principles as described by Biestek in 1961;

- confidentiality is the preservation of secret or private information concerning the user of services, which is disclosed in the professional relationship;

- confidentiality is a basic human right (now defined under the Data Protection Act (1998);

- confidentiality is an ethical obligation of the worker;

- confidentiality is necessary to promote effective working.

However:

- the service user's right to confidentiality is not absolute;

- written permission from the service user is required to divulge their information to other agencies.

Higham (2006, p120) states that:

> The availability of information on the Internet and through computerized records makes confidentiality a threatened principle. Shared confidentiality with legal safeguards is more typical of today's practice. Social workers are not individual therapists, but work within agencies where the requirement to protect vulnerable individuals can conflict with the confidences of service users.

As a tutor working with students I have seen further opportunities where confidentiality has been compromised through email threads, Facebook and other social media sites.

ACTIVITY 5.4

An older service user you are working with tells you she hears arguments from the couple living next door and screams from a child followed by low sobbing noises that carry on a long time into the night. She is afraid that the man might be violent to her if he knows that she has reported this so she asks you to keep it to yourself.

What are the considerations that guide the different courses of action you could take and what might be the consequences for you, the older service user, the parents and children next door?

COMMENT

You will need to be open with your current service user. You will be aware of preserving your relationship with her and also protecting her from any potential repercussions from

Continued

---

the neighbour when you refer the case for investigation. You will need to point out that you now have a duty to report the information to your superior.

You might suggest that your service user should make an anonymous report to the police herself. However, as she is the next-door neighbour you know it is likely the family will soon suspect her.

You might discuss any potential action with your supervisor or colleagues. This will make sure you log your concerns so that you can demonstrate you were accountable.

You will be thinking critically about the impact upon the family of having such an investigation. Perhaps there is a logical explanation. The child may have a physiological condition that needs immediate attention so the father shouts for emergency assistance. The effect of this on the child is that s/he makes noises that sound like she is in pain to the neighbour. You will need to be sensitive as you refer the case and use your legitimate authority cautiously without buying in to the neighbour's view of the situation. Essentially you will be basing your decisions on the most powerless in the situation – the child and her protection.

Whichever line of action you take it will probably cause you some sleepless nights. Thinking through the consequences of your refuting the rights to confidentiality on this sort of occasion will bother you like a critical fly . . . at least if you are a virtuous social worker!

Pre-empting the thorny issue of confidentiality is often a more transparent way of working. By saying at the beginning of contact that you will respect an individual's right to have their details kept private with the following exceptions . . . does feel more honest. However, does it close down a relationship before it has even begun, making your interactions slow and obstructed?

Linda Briskman writes that within contemporary social work, as well as the incursions of the internet and social media, social workers operate across professional boundaries, keep case files electronically and often share information on service users with other services. This can render the need for confidentiality obsolete in the name of having a 'duty of care' and the 'rights' of individuals can only be challenged through consumer organisations. This erosion of confidentiality can be seen in the statement from the International Federation of Social Work in 2002:

> *Social workers should maintain confidentiality regarding information about people who use their services. Exceptions to this may only be justified on the basis of a greater ethical requirement (such as the preservation of life).*

(Briskman, 2004, p55)

As soon as the word 'exceptions' arises this brings into question transparency regarding 'human rights, social justice and advocacy', for no absolute answer can address every unique human situation.

Confidentiality in the practice portfolio

Briefly, there are some rules to observe in the evidence you use for inclusion in your practice portfolio. Remember that this is likely to be read by a Practice Panel, containing academic members of staff, practice educators and agency training personnel. It is likely that they might be able to recognise the service users and carers because:

- they receive services from their agency;

- their case is unique within the practice educator's area of expertise;

- their case is unique within the broader area, e.g. within Greater Manchester or Cumbria;

- their case has reached the attention of the media;

- the reader or member of the Panel personally knows them.

Have a look at **http://cw.routledge.com/textbooks/9780415499125/downloads/ 30-portfolio.pdf** which gives examples of how material is represented in the portfolio (based on an example from Sheffield Hallam University). You will note that even the agency is anonymised in some text.

Here is a checklist for you to reference your documentation and evidence against.

- The placement agency should be referred to as X. You might want to contextualise this, e.g. the placement is a small voluntary agency working with ex-offenders in the south-east of England.

- Names of student, practice educator (on- or off-site) and where applicable the on-site supervisors should be given as initials or a pseudonym.

- All service users, their families, carers, neighbours, etc. should be given as initials. You might consider whether to indicate the gender of these. It might be important to do so, in which case you would use Mr, Mrs, Ms or Miss.

- Use staff initials only, in your own and other agencies.

- Use roles, e.g. the approved social worker, the consultant psychiatrist.

- Academic texts should be referenced in full using name of author(s), dates, book titles and place of publication and publishers.

- Names of hospitals may be referred to by initials, e.g. ROH (local hospital).

- National organisations may be referred to in full, e.g. Citizens Advice, People First.

- You must not use liquid paper to eliminate identifying details on original texts that you then include in the portfolio. If you must anonymise originals then photocopy the document after using liquid paper to block out text. Otherwise the original text can be read through the liquid paper if held up to the light.

As a double-check, re-read the whole portfolio for any lapses in confidentiality before submitting it.

ACTIVITY **5.5**

ACTIVITY **5.5**

Have a look at this submission and see if you can spot any lapses in this student's account.

'My placement was in the adult safeguarding team in Newtown. The team consisted of six staff one of whom was my practice educator, Julie Bedlington. She was working towards her Stage Two practice educator award.

I undertook work with six families, one of which was very problematic and which caused me to question my ability to handle such a complex case. Julie and I had many supervision sessions focusing on risk, as the children of Sonia and Ahmed, Kayten and Rita, were failing to thrive and neighbours reported they were often left alone for long periods. Their locality was within a largely Bangladeshi community with a school and nursery also consisting of mainly minority ethnic children. Ahmed's father is the local Muslim leader – Imam – and the family is expected to conform to the ways of the community; this is causing problems between Sonia and Ahmed.

Ahmed has a conviction for violent behaviour and has been known to be violent towards Sonia. Sonia is taking anti-depressants and expresses thoughts of ending her life and that of her children. Her GP, Dr Kelly, has referred her to a counsellor.'

COMMENT

You will have picked up that there is much of an identifiable nature here. While it is necessary to include this information, the way in which it is expressed goes a long way towards exposing this family, their community and its leader.

People from ethnic minority communities, e.g. Jewish or Polish, those who experience multiple conditions, e.g. a deaf man aged 23 who has AIDS, or who are prominent in the community, e.g. a local magistrate, may be identifiable even with the safeguards of anonymity. For this reason it should be recognised that anonymity and confidentiality cannot be wholly guaranteed but that every attempt will be made to achieve them. The exception to this in practice, rather than in the portfolio evidence, is where there is a risk of harm to others.

CHAPTER SUMMARY

This chapter has introduced you to the breadth and depth of what constitutes evidence and the concept of anticipatory skills in gathering evidence, and has given you some concrete strategies using models and terms to focus your continuing professional development (CPD). Although this is couched under the heading of 'completing your practice portfolio', there are direct links to your ongoing professional practice. Portfolio development for CPD within your ASYE will be a central part of your professional life and progression.

This is not unusual within other professions too, ensuring that within a technological and fast moving world we ensure that we are offering the most accountable and highly professional practice. Contemporary social

Continued

CHAPTER SUMMARY *continued*

work practice often bends to the latest government initiatives, austerity and shifting service user needs. Yet our ability to bear the emotional content of this is always underpinned by our central tenet of considerations for the oppressed (social constructionism), our application of skills and theoretical approaches and our use of legitimate authority. As Pease (2007) would say, towards 'critical knowledge informed practice'. It is to these areas that we move in Chapter 6.

FURTHER READING

Edmondson, D (2014) *Social Work Practice Learning: A Student Guide*. London: Sage.

This whole book will be useful to students in introducing them to the elements of placement practice. Specifically linked to evidencing practice learning is Chapter 6. The style is highly accessible with well signposted contents enabling the student to dip in and use at various stages appropriately throughout their placement and beyond.

Parker, J (2010) *Effective Practice Learning in Social Work*, 2nd edition. Exeter: Learning Matters.

This book is written specifically for social work students who are about to undertake their practice placement. Beginning with the bedrock of values and anti-oppressive practice in practice learning, the book progresses through highly relevant chapters on integrating theory and reflective practice, using supervision and gathering evidence and demonstrating competence to name a few. The style inducts the reader into activities, case studies and research summaries that are highly effective in promoting CPD.

USEFUL WEBSITES

www.hpc-uk.org

The National Occupational Standards for Social Work (2002) are contained in this lengthy document but you will be in no doubt as to what you need to demonstrate in order to pass your placement! There are helpful statements, derived from consultation with service users and their carers, as to what they expect of a social worker. These will show you the areas of practice you will be tested in. The code of practice for employers and social care workers are outlined and the purpose, roles and elements you are required to fulfil are listed. The performance criteria are very useful if you are wondering what evidence is needed. There is a useful diagram on page 18 showing the links between the key roles and values and ethics.

http://melinabick-socialworkportfolio.yolasite.com/my-practice-framework.php

An innovative way to think about evidencing your portfolio. Of course you do have to follow your university guidelines but it is useful to use such visual imagery to stimulate your creativity. You could include such a method in your appendices.

Chapter 6

Moving on: NQSW, ASYE and all that . . .

This chapter will help you to develop the following capabilities, to the appropriate level, from the Professional Capabilities Framework:

- *Professionalism*: Describe the importance of emotional resilience in social work; describe the importance of personal and professional boundaries.
- *Values and ethics*: Demonstrate awareness of own personal values and how these can impact on practice.
- *Diversity*: Recognise the importance of diversity in human identity and experience, and the application of anti-discriminatory and anti-oppressive principles in social work practice.
- *Critical reflection and analysis*: Recognise and describe why evidence is important in social work practice.

It will also introduce you to the following standards as set out in the 2008 Social Work Subject Benchmark Statement:

4.6   Critically reflect upon ethical principles and dilemmas.
5.1.2 The service delivery context.
5.1.5 The nature of social work practice.
5.5.4 Intervention and evaluation.
6.2   The learning process in social work.
7.3   Knowledge and understanding.

Introduction

This final chapter feels like it is the end of the beginning of your career, rather than the beginning of the end of your studies. In launching on to the next stage of your learning journey you will be continuing many of the habits that you have developed throughout your practice placements and bolstering your aptitudes for learning. One example of this will be your continuing use of a portfolio of evidence products and your reflective, reflexive and critical thinking through a learning journal. Your mentor/supervisor will produce reports on your work that will be used to elevate your professional career through the PCF levels and within the nine domains, way beyond the ASYE. This chapter will give you a flavour of this process and requirements.

Moving on as an NQSW

Congratulations, you have successfully passed your university degree and are looking forward to evenings and weekends with more time to get on with your life! That is true but notice that I did not say 'without any studying'. You are now moving into a year of consolidation, collaboration, creativity, criticality and contribution.

It is likely that you will have obtained a position with an employer who has actively sought an NQSW for the post. Here are some statements by recruiting social work employers.

Posts specifically advertised for NQSWs

The job advertisements below were all taken from **www.indeed.co.uk/Newly-Qualified-Social-Worker-jobs** on 12 August 2014. Have a look at this website for current jobs for NQSWs.

We offer protected caseloads and a comprehensive Assessed and Supported Year in Employment for Newly Qualified Social Workers.

Tameside

We have reduced caseloads across all of our teams; we have achieved our target of average caseloads of 15 on most teams. Newly Qualified Social Workers also have protected caseloads and an extensive training programme in their assessed year of practice.

Essex

Our client based with Camden Council currently has a vacancy for a Family Worker to work in one of their Children Centres Monday to Friday, 35 hours a week. This would be ideal for a Newly Qualified Social Worker.

Camden

If you are newly qualified or this is your first post since qualifying then under the requirements of the Assessed and Supported Year in Employment (ASYE) you will be supported and assessed in your role as registered social worker for a period of one year. Should you fail to meet the required standard and be unable to practise as a social worker the Council will have to consider the termination of your employment.

Oldham

This post is open to both experienced and Newly Qualified Social Workers (NQSWs). NQSWs will be supported to complete the Assessed and Supported

Continued

Continued

> *Year in Employment (ASYE) and their continued employment will be subject to the successful completion of the ASYE programme.*
>
> Stockton-on-Tees
>
> *We do also encourage Newly Qualified Social Workers to apply for this post – please make us aware if you are not HCPC registered as a newly qualified worker.*
>
> Capita resourcing – Birmingham

Having begun your professional life as an NQSW you will be working with your mentor/ supervisor (the equivalent of your practice educator) to evidence your practice development. There are clear guidelines about how you might do this that are set out for your employer and for you and these can be found at: **www.skillsforcare.org.uk/ Social-work/Assessed-and-Supported-Year-in-Employment/The-Assessed-and-Supported-Year-in-Employment-(ASYE).aspx.**

Scroll down and take a look at the ASYE mini guide for NQSWs and the FAQs on this website. There is some very useful guidance on the range, depth and types of evidence you must present, registration and funding, the support you can expect and the decision-making process. Additionally, there are some created case studies of what might constitute evidence for a student completing the ASYE. Click on 'Assessment Case Studies' then 'view the case studies'. These will be good templates to follow.

The support you can expect is also detailed for you:

- supervision every week for the first six weeks;
- thereafter supervision monthly;
- a protected caseload;
- a personal development plan.

Like most of your evidence base for your social work qualification where you had to show how you incorporated the key roles and the HCPC guidance on ethics, in the ASYE you will be compiling a portfolio to evidence your capabilities at the ASYE level of the PCF (see Appendix 1 for the PCF). Throughout the ASYE year you will be expected to engage with all nine areas of the PCF at the level of an NQSW. This means there must be evidence of the following:

- *professionalism;*
- *values and ethics;*
- *diversity;*
- *rights, justice and economic well-being;*

- *knowledge;*

- *critical reflection and analysis;*

- *intervention and skills;*

- *context and organisations;*

- *professional leadership.*

(TCSW, 2012)

Suggested evidence for the ASYE

This should be concise, give an overview of your practice, contain some mentor/ supervisor or staff observations, and meet all nine areas of the PCF at the ASYE level. The evidence needs to be 'sufficient' yet you might find you excel at some of the work where you have a passion. I suggest you relax into the work, enjoy your qualified status, use supervision intelligently and along the way select your evidence. This is so much more enjoyable than focusing wholly on the PCF requirements.

Some of your evidence can be obtained through:

- your reflective log;

- initial, core and risk assessments;

- formal written reports and letters;

- duty team – working under pressure;

- collaborative meetings with multi-professional and multi-agency groups;

- facilitating service user groups;

- facilitating staff group meetings, minute taking and chairing;

- making in-house presentations;

- recording on the management information system;

- conducting case planning and review meetings and recording these;

- seeking evaluation of your performance from staff, service users and other professionals;

- records of supervision;

- photographs of planned activities with service users (with their permission);

- examples of products you have produced, e.g. service user guides, action research outputs completed by you;

- outputs to evidence your contextualising of the legal process of your work;

- critique of agency documents and pro formas.

This list is not exhaustive and you can use anything generated by you or in conjunction with others, so long as you demonstrate and explain your part. Try to be creative in gathering your evidence and discuss it with your mentor/supervisor, as they might need to sign it off.

Most employers of NQSWs have developed a 'guided tour' of learning activity courses to support you through the process. Have a look at the courses available for the ASYE year at the Somerset Centre for Integrated Learning: **www.scilearning.org.uk/courses** – just click on the ASYE links.

Linking the ASYE evidence to critical events

While it is easy to become drawn into a functionalist or technical rationalist culture due to the high pressure experienced in some agencies I want to suggest that by holding firm onto a critical stance you will be able to provide much of the evidence needed in successfully completing your ASYE. Here is a case study of Ellie, a social worker dealing with an ongoing difficulty in her work environment.

CASE STUDY **6.1**

I had been working with service users with learning disabilities with psychological needs that required intensive behavioural management. Perhaps because of the need to deal with service users with challenging behaviour, my team consisted mainly of male staff. I found working in a male-dominated team very trying. I grew tired of some of the comments and sexist assumptions that were commonly made. On many occasions I witnessed an oppressive use of language about women, for example 'boys will be boys, but one day all girls will be women' and 'why do women have small feet – so they can get closer to the sink'. All this used in a joking way and involving service users.

Action taken – After much reflection I decided to do some research on the notions of feminine and masculine roles using a lens of liberal feminism. As I began to understand the roots of womanhood – domesticity, and manliness – wage earning and public presence, I realised how this was being played out in a gendered organisational culture. I began to see how the males were being disadvantaged in the organisation by being stereotyped as the ones to deal with challenging behaviour, e.g. rational, tough, decision oriented, strategic and analytic, whereas females were victims of stereotypes of traditional roles of inferiority. When I tried to break out of this role I was accused of being 'overly assertive' and trying to 'play the male role'.

Output – I asked to meet with the whole team to explain how I thought the male/female stereotypes were impacting on us all and preventing the team from moving forward. Two of the male staff approached me afterwards to ask how they could work with me to put on some training, as they were shocked to realise how their behaviour had affected me. As a result I led a team of four staff members, two male and two female, to prepare and deliver a short course to a group of self-selecting staff and service users.

Continued

CASE STUDY 6.1 continued

Evidence attached:

- *outline plan and programme delivery of 4 × 1 hour sessions;*

- *evaluation comments from participants;*

- *evaluation comments from the planning and delivery team re my performance.*

ASYE elements covered:

- *professionalism;*

- *values and ethics;*

- *rights and justice;*

- *knowledge;*

- *critical reflection and analysis;*

- *contexts and organisations;*

- *professional leadership.*

Signed off by Mentor/Supervisor

This short narrative has covered most of the ASYE requirements, and has evidenced the worker's capacity to reflect and learn and drive this new knowledge forward in a positive way to change the organisation for the better. This is just one example and more would be needed, as it is the sustained ability to practise that is required. However, it does show that one piece of evidence can be used in a variety of ways, just as you did in completing your portfolio under the key roles while on placement.

Portfolio tasks linked to technical rationalism

Although I advocate a critical and reflexive (and where possible transformative) approach to your practice, I see this as leading, infusing and reflecting upon the necessary technical rationalist aspects of the work. Practice must deal with the managerial aspects of the role of social work. It must work to and reflect the requirements of legal processes, be accountable, inform funding processes and constantly evaluate its effectiveness, diversity and the well-being of service users and their community. In order to do this, procedures, forms, guidance and protocols need to be followed. Remember Pease (2007) – in his book *Critical Theory Meets Evidence Based Practice*, he uses the phrase 'critical knowledge informed practice' in recognition of the fact that critical realism has to exist to bring the two binaries of criticality and technicality within the human sphere that is social work. Some agencies give guidance on the types of management documentation that they see as being commensurate with the ASYE, for example, within referral and assessment activities to:

- complete two children and families assessments, one of which is then closed, no further action, and one which you are recommending goes on for a full assessment;
- identify the risk and protective factors in both cases in relation to all the children/ young people in the house using the risk assessment pro forma;
- list the agencies you have contacted to build your evidence;
- complete the 'child(ren)'s wishes and views' pro forma;
- include your signed supervision notes indicating your evidence for closing or retaining the case (both you and mentor to sign);
- complete a chronology of both families;
- list the legal framework, policies, guidance and the theory(ies) used;
- attend relevant training courses appropriate to your work.

To add the critical aspects of your practice you need to overlay a critical lens to:

- demonstrate your ability to assess the implications of failure to take any action, to use alternative theories, or to fail to apply the principle of least intervention;
- critically discern any dilemmas and tensions in the work;
- identify any gaps in provision for these families;
- identify any areas of training needed for your personal development.

This type of evidencing practice will continue throughout your career and will form the basis of good habits in proving your capability in whatever sphere of social work you enter.

Continuing professional development as a career requirement

As with most professions, continuing professional development (CPD) is required to evidence that you are up-to-date, actively engaged with the contested and shifting nature of social work and enhancing your skills to better serve those who use services and your agency.

After passing your ASYE (your mentor may issue a pass or fail), you will be required to maintain your professional registration with the HCPC every two years. Your employer will give you guidance as to what practice activities are representative of the various levels. For example, after gaining experience and consolidating your expertise you might choose to specialise in becoming one of the following:

- professional social work educator;
- advanced social work practitioner;
- social work manager;

- strategic social work manager;
- principal social worker;
- strategic social work educator.

The nine areas of the PCF still apply, as will the requirement to maintain your HCPC registration.

Although you may feel at this point that having to prove yourself through providing evidence and being monitored will weigh heavily on your professional life, this framework has been created to give clear pathways for your ongoing professional development. It provides clarity for employers too, who will need to represent how they are supporting their staff in their workforce returns to government.

CHAPTER SUMMARY

Moving into qualified practice will be an exciting time for you at a time when the profile of social work has been considerably elevated with the formation of the HCPC, SCIE, The College of Social Work, the Social Work Reform Board, Skills for Care and the Centre for Workforce Intelligence. To supplement this wealth of resource material your agency will have actively recruited you because you are an NQSW and agreed a support plan in conjunction with a mentor/supervisor. The stage is set for your career trajectory and I hope that this book has helped to prepare you for a successful and rewarding vocation.

FURTHER READING

Keen, S, Gray, I, Parker, J, Galpin, D and Brown, K (2009) *Newly Qualified Social Workers: A Handbook for Practice.* Exeter: Learning Matters.

An essential book for NQSWs covering the management of transitions, induction, probation and supervision. Chapter 5 would be particularly relevant to reassure new social workers in that it deals with how to thrive in social work. The style links to useful activities and to the key roles of the National Occupational Standards for Social Work. There are useful contributions from service users, carers and NQSWs.

Edmondson, D (2014) *Social Work Practice Learning: A Student Guide.* London: Sage.

Chapter 10 looks at moving from the end of our course into the ASYE. There is guidance on applying for your first post and undertaking the interview. Importantly the final message is about 'looking after yourself' – a note to take care of your own physical and psychological well-being.

Bogg, D and Challis, M (2013) *Evidencing CPD: A Guide to Building Your Social Work Portfolio.* St Albans: Critical Publishing Limited.

A book written especially for the social work placements and beyond. The context of portfolio work is set in place with a useful section on how the portfolios will be assessed. Students seem to have found the book very helpful according to their reviews.

USEFUL WEBSITES

www.scie.org.uk/publications/nqswtool/index.asp

Part of the Social Care Institute for Excellence website, this page gives access to resources to support NQSWs in their ASYE. The resources are grouped according to the NQSW outcome statements.

www.skillsforcare.org.uk/Social-work/Assessed-and-Supported-Year-in-Employment/Gathering-feedback/Gathering-feedback-from-people-in-need-of-care-and-support.aspx

This page gives access to a range of resources and tools that have been developed to assist NQSWs and their assessors to gather and use feedback from a range of service users.

www.youtube.com/embed/OHBU_lyaRX4?autoplay=1

Vox pop of NQSWs and other stakeholders in the ASYE process talking about their experiences.

Appendix 1

Professional Capabilities Framework

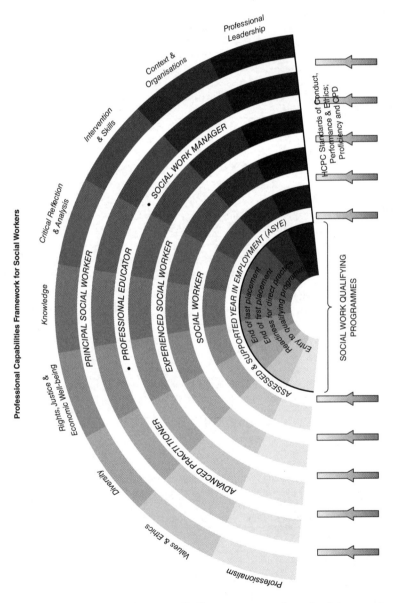

Professional Capabilities Framework for Social Workers

Professional Leadership

Context & Organisations

Intervention & Skills

Critical Reflection & Analysis

Knowledge

Rights, Justice & Economic Well-being

Diversity

Values & Ethics

Professionalism

PRINCIPAL SOCIAL WORKER

PROFESSIONAL EDUCATOR

EXPERIENCED SOCIAL WORKER

SOCIAL WORK MANAGER

SOCIAL WORKER

ASSESSED & SUPPORTED YEAR IN EMPLOYMENT (ASYE)

ADVANCED PRACTITIONER

End of last placement
End of first placement
Readiness for direct practice
Entry to qualifying programme

HCPC Standards of Conduct, Performance & Ethics; Proficiency and CPD

SOCIAL WORK QUALIFYING PROGRAMMES

Professional Capabilities Framework diagram reproduced with permission of The College of Social Work

Appendix 2
Ladder of Citizen Participation

Ladder of Participation

Degree of citizen power		
CITIZEN CONTROL	Stakeholders have the idea, set up the project and come to facilitators for advice, discussion and support. Facilitators do not direct, but offer advice for citizens to consider.
DELEGATED POWER	The goal is likely to have been set by the facilitator but the resources and responsibility for solving the problem are passed to the stakeholders. There are clear lines of accountability and two-way communication with those giving away the power.
PARTNERSHIP	Stakeholders have direct involvement in the decision making process and actioning the decision. Each stakeholder has a clear role, set of responsibilities and powers – usually to achieve a shared common goal. Two-way communication is vital.

Degree of tokenism

PLACATION	Stakeholders have an active role as shapers of opinions, ideas and outcomes, but the final decision remains with the facilitators. Two-way communication is essential.
CONSULTATION	Stakeholders' opinions and views are sought through various means, but final decisions are made by those doing the consulting.
INFORMING	Stakeholders are kept informed of what is going on, but are not offered the opportunity to contribute themselves. Communication is one way.

Non-participation

THERAPY	
MANIPULATION	To educate or cure the stakeholders. The idea is defined and the participation is aimed only to gain public support. 'If we educate the stakeholders, they will change their ill-informed attitudes and they will support our plans.'

Adapted from Sherry Arnstein's Ladder of Citizen Participation, www.ice.org.uk

References

Adams, R, Dominelli, L and Payne, M (2009a) *Social Work Themes, Issues and Critical Debates*, 3rd edition. Basingstoke: Palgrave Macmillan.

Adams, R, Dominelli, L and Payne, M (2009b) *Critical Practice in Social Work*, 2nd edition. Basingstoke: Palgrave Macmillan.

Adams, R, Dominelli, L and Payne, M (eds) (2009c) *Practising Social Work in a Complex World*. London: Palgrave Macmillan.

Archer, M, Baskar, R, Collier, A, Lawson, T and Norrie, A (eds) (1998) *Critical Realism: Essential Readings*. London: Routledge.

Arnstein, S (1969 original publication date) Diagram accessed at www.debitage.net on 5 July 2014.

Barnett, R (1997) *Higher Education: A Critical Business*. Buckinghamshire: The Society for Research into Higher Education and Open University Press.

Benner, P (2004) Using the Dreyfus model of skill acquisition to describe and interpret skill acquisition and clinical judgement in nursing practice and education. *Bulletin of Science, Technology and Society*, 24 (3), 188.

Bourdieu, P, Loic, J and Wacquant, D (1992) *An Invitation to Reflexive Sociology*. Chicago: University of Chicago Press.

Braye, S and Preston-Shoot, M (2008) *Empowering Practice in Social Care*. Berkshire: Oxford University Press.

Briskman, L (2004) Pushing ethical boundaries for children and families. In R Adams, L Dominelli and M Payne (eds), *Critical Practice in Social Work*, 2nd edition. Basingstoke: Palgrave Macmillan.

Butler-Sloss, E (1988) *Report of the Inquiry into Child Abuse in Cleveland 1987*, Cm 412. London: HMSO.

Care Council for Wales (2012) *Supervising and Appraising Well: A Guide to Effective Supervision and Appraisal for Those Working in Social Care*.

Carson, G (2010) *Community Care*. Online. Accessed 23 January 2013 from http://www.communitycare.co.uk/2010/09/21/social-work-degree-placements-explained

Cree, V and Wallace, SJ (2009) Risk and protection: working with children and families. In R Adams, L Dominelli and M Payne (eds), *Practising Social Work in a Complex World*. London: Palgrave Macmillan.

Dempsey, M, Murphy, M and Halton, C (2008) Introducing tools of reflective learning into peer supervision groups in a social work agency: An action research project. *Journal of Practice Teaching and Learning*, 8 (2), 25–43. London: Whiting and Birch.

Department of Health (2008) *Human Rights Inquiry: Executive Summary*. London: HMSO.

Dreyfus, S (2004) The five-stage model of adult skill acquisition. *Bulletin of Science, Technology and Society*, 24 (3), 177–81.

Dunk-West, P (2013) *How to be a Social Worker*. Basingstoke: Palgrave Macmillan.

Edmondson, D (2014) *Social Work Practice Learning: A Student Guide*. London: Sage.

Flap, H and Volker, B (2001) Social networks. *An International Journal of Structural Analysis*, 23 (4), 297–320. Elsevier BV 2013.

Fook, J (2002) *Social Work: Critical Theory and Practice*. London: Sage.

Forrester, D (2011) Evaluation research. In M Gray, J Midgley and S Webb (eds), *The Sage International Handbook for Social Work Research*. London: Sage.

Fortune, AE and Abramson, JS (2008) Predictors of satisfaction with field practicum among social work students (pp95–110). Published online at: www.tandfonline.com/doi/abs/10.1300/J001v11n01_07#.UjwO0BbIbmY

Goleman, D (1998) *Working with Emotional Intelligence*. London: Bloomsbury Publishing Plc.

Gould, N and Baldwin, M (2004) *Social Work, Critical Reflection and the Learning Organisation*. Aldershot: Ashgate.

Higham, P (2006) *Social Work: Introducing Professional Practice*. London: Sage.

Howe, D (2008) *The Emotionally Intelligent Social Worker*. Basingstoke: Palgrave Macmillan.

IFSW (International Federation of Social Work) (2014) http://ifsw.org/policies/definition-of-social-work

Ingram, R (2012) Locating emotional intelligence at the heart of social work practice. *British Journal of Social Work*. First published online: 3 April 2012, http://bjsw.oxfordjournals.org

Ingram, R (2013) Exploring emotions within formal and informal forums: messages from social work practitioners. *British Journal of Social Work*. First published online: 14 October 2013, http://bjsw.oxfordjournals.org

Jenkins, R (1982) Pierre Bourdieu and the reproduction of determinism. *Sociology*, 16, 270–81.

Jones, S (2013) *Critical Learning for Social Work Students*, 2nd edition. London: Sage.

Jordan, B (2004) Emancipatory social work: opportunity or oxymoron? *British Journal of Social Work*, 34 (1), 5–19.

Jung, CG (1989) *Psychology and Religion: West and East*, 2nd edition (RFC Hull Translation). Princeton: Princeton University Press.

MacAlister, J (2012) *Frontline: Improving the Children's Social Work Profession*. London: IPPR.

Masterson, SS, Lewis, K, Goldman, BM and Taylor, MS (2000) Integrating justice and social exchange: the differing effects of fair procedures and treatment on work relationships. *Journal of Academy of Management*, 43 (4), 738–48.

May-Chahal, C (2010) *Community Care*. Online. Accessed 23 January 2013 from http://www.communitycare.co.uk/2010/09/20/why-social-work-degree-placements-are-important

McBeath, G and Webb, SA (2002) Virtue ethics and social work: being lucky, realistic and not doing one's duty. *British Journal of Social Work*, 32 (8), 1015–36. Oxford Journals.

Megele, C (2008) A social work student reflects on her placement. Published online: www.socialworkconnections.org.uk/features/158/a_social_work_student_reflects_on_her_placements.

Munro, E (2011) *The Munro Review of Child Protection: Final Report*. London: HMSO.

NIHCE (2011) Service user experience in adult mental health: improving the experience of care for people using adult NHS mental health services.

Parker, J (2010) *Effective Practice Learning in Social Work*, 2nd edition. Exeter: Learning Matters.

Payne, M (2005) *Modern Social Work Theory*, 3rd edition. Basingstoke: Palgrave Macmillan.

Pease, B (2007) *Critical Social Work Theory Meets Evidence Based Practice in Australia: Towards Critical Knowledge-Informed Practice in Social Work*. Kyoto-shi Japan: Sekai Shisosha.

Pease, B and Fook, J (1999) *Transforming Social Work Practice: Postmodern Critical Perspectives*. London and New York: Routledge.

Phillipson, J (2009) Supervision and being supervised. In R Adams, L Dominelli and M Payne (eds), *Practising Social Work in a Complex World*. London: Palgrave Macmillan.

Podolny, JM and Baron, JN (1997) Resources and relationships: social networks and mobility in the workplace. *American Sociological Review*, 62 (October), 673–93.

Saleebey, D (1995) The strengths perspective in social work practice: extensions and cautions. *Social Work: A Journal of the National Association of Social Workers*, 41 (3), 296–305. NASW Press. Oxford Journals.

Shusterman, R (ed.) (1999) *Bourdieu: A Critical Reader*. Oxford: Blackwell.

Social Work Reform Board (2012) *The Assessed and Supported Year in Employment for Newly Qualified Social Workers*. Online: www.skillsforcare.org.uk/asye

Somerset Centre for Integrated Learning (2013/14) *Newly Qualified Social Workers Assessed and Supported Year in Practice*.

TCSW (The College of Social Work) (2012) *Domains within the Professional Capabilities Framework*. Online: www.tcsw.org.uk/pcf.aspx

Topps (2002) *The National Occupational Standards for Social Work*. Online: www.hpc-uk.org

Vanlaere, L, Bouckaert, F and Gastmans, C (2007) Care for suicidal older people: current clinical-ethical considerations. *Journal of Medical Ethics*, 33 (7). BMJ Journals, available at www.ncbi.nlm.nih.gov

Index